DETRO

Tigers

GONE
WILD

MISCHIEF, CRIMES & HARD TIME

GEORGE HUNTER

THE
History
PRESS

Published by The History Press
Charleston, SC
www.historypress.com

Unless otherwise noted, all photos are courtesy of the *Detroit News*.

First published 2020

Manufactured in the United States

ISBN 9781467143295

Library of Congress Control Number: 2019954267

Notice: The information in this book is true and complete to the best of our knowledge. It is offered without guarantee on the part of the author or The History Press. The author and The History Press disclaim all liability in connection with the use of this book.

To my wife, Lynn: You shine a beautiful light into my life.
To my son, Daniel: Always my little buddy-buddy, no matter how big you get.
To Mom and Charles: You guided me through the tough times and provided an
example of the right way to live.
To Steve, Shawn, Kim and my late brother, Tony.
To my father-in-law, Jerry, and my late mother-in-law, Bev.
And to all the rest of my family.
I love you all.

CONTENTS

PREFACE

Detroit, crime and turmoil go together like Tram, Lou and Sparky. The Detroit Tigers Baseball Club, like the city it represents, has a history fraught with fury and felony. While bad actors certainly don't represent the majority of Detroiters or those who played (and rooted) for the Tigers, ne'er-do-wells, lawbreakers and general chaos have always been an unavoidable, crucial, fascinating part of the story.

Focusing on the foibles of Detroit and its ball club in no way suggests other teams and cities haven't had their fair share of troubles. But when it comes to lawbreaking and bedlam, the Tigers and Detroit have had particularly colorful histories.

What other major-league team signed a star player out of prison? The Tigers did it twice, snatching up Ron LeFlore from Jackson Prison and Gates Brown from the Ohio penitentiary that was later used in the movie *The Shawshank Redemption*. Detroit's greatest player, Ty Cobb, stabbed a hotel employee, one of several times he ran afoul of the law during his brilliant and tumultuous—and often mischaracterized—career.

Ex-Tigers have done prison time for crimes ranging from armed robbery to racketeering—and worse. A former relief pitcher tried to set a group of men on fire and dismember them with a machete after they'd kidnaped his mother. An ex-infielder threatened to blow up a cruise ship unless he was paid a sizeable ransom. And while LeFlore and Brown went from prison to baseball, star pitcher Denny McLain's life took the opposite trajectory.

On the diamond, the Tigers have been involved in their share of epic brawls that often ended with arrests. In the stands, Tiger fans were no angels themselves, displaying a world-famous penchant for throwing things at ballplayers and fighting each other. General manager Jim Campbell shut down the bleachers in the 1980s because of rowdiness, drunkenness and open marijuana smoking, making him the heir to a long line of Tiger officials who also lamented the bleacherites' behavior.

One of the most infamous sports riots in U.S. history raged outside Tiger Stadium following the team's 1984 World Series win. Away from home, the Tigers were in the thick of such debacles as Disco Demolition Night in Chicago and the first player strike in baseball history, staged by Cobb's teammates after he stormed into the stands in New York and thrashed a verbally abusive fan.

In the early days of baseball, the game was infiltrated by gamblers, and the Tigers weren't immune. While the Chicago White Sox lay claim to baseball's most explosive gambling scandal by throwing the 1919 World Series, Detroit has had its share of bombshell gambling controversies, along with rumors of fixed Series games involving the Tigers that persist more than a century later. McLain was suspended from baseball for having ties to a Mafia gambling ring.

The vast majority of people who played and rooted for the Detroit Tigers are to be celebrated. However, by lifting the rock and peering at the dark side, perhaps it allows us to better appreciate the good things the Motor City Kitties have offered through the years, from Charlie Gehringer to Curtis Granderson.

And, let's be honest, in Detroit, isn't rooting for bad boys a time-honored tradition?

1

BORN ROWDY

The Detroit Tigers and their fans came out of the womb scratching and snarling.

The sport of "base ball"—a synthesis of children's bat-and-ball games like rounders and old cat—evolved in New York in the mid-nineteenth century. The New York Knickerbockers codified the first official rules in 1845 and the following year played the first recorded game, in which the New York Nine thrashed the Knicks, 23–1, at Hoboken, New Jersey's Elysian Fields.

The new game meandered its way westward to Detroit about five years later. For the next forty years, the future Motor City was represented by a string of amateur and minor-league clubs that popped up and petered out.

In 1881, Detroit was awarded a National League franchise, the Wolverines, which won a world championship in 1887 before folding a year later. The team's owner was Detroit's mayor, William G. Thompson, a Civil War veteran who was full of piss and vinegar. He once got into a bloody fight with his brother-in-law, Daniel Campeau, inside the old Michigan Central Railroad depot. Most of the blood was Thompson's. The beatdown was reported by newspapers across the country, including the *New York Times*, which opined: "The affair is the talk of the town, and public sympathy is altogether on Campeau's side." In 1891, after his tenure as mayor, Thompson was involved in another high-profile brawl that ended with a shooting outside a downtown Detroit bar.

The current Tiger franchise began in 1894 as a minor-league club in the Western League. The team played in League Park at Helen and Champlain

The Wolverines, Detroit's first major-league baseball team, played at Recreation Park, which was near the site of the Detroit Medical Center.

(now Lafayette) on Detroit's east side before moving to Michigan and Trumbull in 1896. Their new home was Bennett Park, situated directly across the street from the Trumbull Detroit Police precinct. The close proximity to the cop shop proved to be a blessing—the short distance saved wear and tear on the officers' shoes as they regularly beat a path across the street to quell violence before, during or after ball games.

A year after moving to "The Corner," Tiger fans staged a riot on Opening Day, and the umpire was lucky to escape Bennett Park without serious injury. The trouble started in the ninth inning of a 4–4 game against the Indianapolis Indians when umpire Buck Ebright called Tiger left fielder Hercules Burnett out on a close play at second base.

"In less than a minute the umpire was surrounded by 18 or more wildly excited players," the *Detroit News* reported. "They brandished their fists under his nose, called him every name not in the dictionary, and made his life a burden. Ebright stalked around like a man in a dream. He did not know what to do or how to do it."

The umpire knew enough to fine Burnett and another player twenty-five dollars apiece and throw them out of the game. Burnett refused to obey the ump's order to leave the ballpark; instead, he sat on the bench the rest of the game, screaming things like "I'll punch your face" and threatening to break the umpire's nose, according to the *News*.

Detroit lost in ten innings. After the game, the umpire was standing near the Indianapolis players' bench when the Tiger outfielder attacked him in full view of the stands.

"Burnett walked over and without warning commenced to rain blows upon Ebright's head and shoulders," the *News* reported. "He hit him three or four times before the players interfered and dragged the furious Detroiter away. The crowd became wildly excited. There were cries of 'Slug him,' 'Kill the umpire,' 'Put a rope around his neck,' etc."

Fans scaled the fence and crowded around the umpire. Two Detroit cops tried to fend off the enraged crowd.

"The policeman and his charge were surrounded by an angry mob," the *News* said. "One enthusiastic fan managed to swat the umpire a heavy blow in the back of the neck. A second policeman grabbed him. The crowd surrounded the copper and made things so lively that he let his man go."

Rickety "wildcat" bleachers in Detroit predate the Tigers' move to Michigan and Trumbull. Here, fans stand on a dilapidated grandstand to get a free peek at the action during a game at Boulevard Park, the team's original home at the corner of Lafayette and Helen Streets.

"The Indianapolis players surrounded the policeman and the umpire and by a lively swinging of their bats kept the crowd at bay until Ebright was hustled into the bus," the *News* said. "Ebright, afraid of more missiles, crouched in the bottom. The Indianapolis players piled in, the driver whipped up his horses, and the bus tore down the street. The mob did not discover where Ebright was hidden for a moment. Then they gave chase. It would have fared worse with Ebright had they caught him."

During an era when sportswriters were openly partisan toward the home team, the *Free Press* blamed the Tiger player for the insurrection. "Burnett's ruffianly action had incited the bleacherites to a high pitch," the paper said.

The Opening Day riot of 1897 established a precedent for rowdiness at the corner of Michigan and Trumbull that would last for generations.

IN 1900, THE WESTERN League changed its name to the American League, although it would still be another year before the circuit would be considered a major league. That same year, Detroit businessman and landowner James D. Burns purchased the Tiger franchise for $12,000. The blustery Burns would later be elected Wayne County sheriff, although, during his tenure as Tiger owner, he had no problem manipulating the law—and sometimes breaking it—to get his way.

On August 4, 1900, Burns used his considerable influence to have *Chicago American* sportswriter Sherman Duffy arrested in the Bennett Park press box during a game against the Chicago White Sox. His "crime"? He wrote a story that ticked Burns off, so the Tiger owner had the reporter thrown in jail on criminal libel charges.

It's the only known instance in American sports history in which a journalist was arrested in the press box while covering a game because a team owner didn't like his article.

A pair of Wayne County Sheriff's deputies "did not even give the newspaper man a chance to finish scoring the game, but took him...to jail and locked him up," the *News* reported.

Duffy's "criminally libelous" article appeared in the July 15, 1900 edition of the *American*, a day after Tiger fans had started yet another riot at Bennett Park. The bleacherites were angry about some of the calls made by umpire Joe Cantillon. So, after the 4–2 Tiger loss, dozens of rowdy fans rushed the field, threatening to tear the hapless ump to pieces.

The cops from the Trumbull Precinct were dispatched to the familiar trouble spot across the street. The constables formed a cordon around

A mounted Detroit police officer engaging in crowd control in Navin Field on Opening Day 1926. Police were often called to quell disturbances at the corner of Michigan and Trumbull in the team's early days.

Cantillon and escorted him to the nearby Barclay Hotel. Several dozen fans hung around outside the hotel for hours, hollering threats until their throats presumably gave out.

Duffy's piece in the Chicago paper decried the "disgraceful assault on an umpire…by the players and spectators.…[The] owner and manager of the Detroit club [were] responsible for the insult of the official."

Enraged, Burns sued the reporter and his newspaper. In the Wayne County Circuit Court filing, which sought $10,000 in damages, Burns proclaimed that the accusations in the offending article were "maliciously and wrongfully made; that [Burns] was not responsible for, and did not incite the spectators…that the spectators…were not disreputable or disorderly persons, but were persons of respectable, intelligent and refined people of the city of Detroit."

After the suit was filed, Burns bided his time until the White Sox returned to Detroit. They arrived on Thursday, August 2, but the vindictive Tiger owner waited until that Saturday before having Wayne County Sheriff's deputies P.J. Hayes and Theodore Cicotte storm the Bennett Park press box during the game and place the sportswriter under arrest. According to the *News*, Burns asked the cops to postpone the arrest until after the courts closed on Saturday at 4:00 p.m. so Duffy would have to languish in the Wayne County Jail until Monday morning. But the scribe was locked up only about six hours before Wayne County Circuit Court judge George S. Hosmer learned of the farce and released him on $500 bond.

American League president Ban Johnson was furious at the Tiger owner. "The arrest was a malicious act on the part of Burns," he said. "It will kill him in baseball, and every lover of clean ballplaying, fair dealing, and all that goes to make the national game what it has been, the best of sports, should cry him down."

The libel suit was eventually dropped.

MANY AMERICAN CITIES AT the turn of the twentieth century had religious-based "blue laws" on the books that prohibited playing baseball on Sunday. Tiger owners thumbed their noses at the law and staged ball games anyway—and the drunken, rowdy Detroit fans who attended these outlaw Sunday games handed plenty of ammunition to the prohibitionists.

The Tigers initially got around the blue laws by playing Sunday games in Mount Clemens and River Rouge, suburban municipalities that weren't as stringent about enforcement as Detroit, which had a powerful ministers' lobby. After Burns bought the team, he moved Sunday games to property his family owned at Dix and Waterman in Springwells Township, which was later annexed into Detroit and now cuts through the center of the city's southwest side.

Just before the 1900 season, Burns hired a crew to hurriedly construct Burns Park, a rickety wood facility that seated between twenty-five hundred and three thousand fans. The park was built on a parcel near the city's stockyards, and the foul stench from the yards reflected the mood of the fans.

Fights constantly broke out before, during and after games at Burns Park. The violence fueled the concerns of Detroit's ministers, who complained loudly and often about the sin of grown men chasing baseballs—and cracking skulls—on the Sabbath.

Tiger batboy George "Pat" Dery told the *Detroit News* that Sunday games at Burns Park "invariably ended in a free-for-all." His job entailed scooping up the bats quickly after games ended, because, he said, "the fewer bats, the fewer broken bones."

The Tiger owner knew how violent the patrons of his namesake ballpark could be. On July 15, 1900, Burns forfeited a game against the Cleveland Blues because he thought the crowd might attack the umpire—although he appeared more worried about his Sunday profits than the ump's well-being.

The game was played a day after umpire Cantillon's close call had sparked the on-field donnybrook that prompted Duffy, the *Chicago American* sportswriter, to file a column that would land him in the Wayne County Jail on criminal libel charges. Cantillon was scheduled to be the lone umpire for the next game against Cleveland, but Burns wouldn't have it.

"Burns notified [American League president Johnson] that another umpire would be necessary for the Sunday game with Cleveland, as there was no police protection at Burns Park, and the feeling of the crowd against Cantillon was so strong that he feared the official's presence at the grounds might lead to a riot and result in killing Sunday baseball," the *News* reported.

The two teams played anyway, with Tiger catcher Lewis "Sport" McAllister acting as sit-in umpire. The Tigers beat Cleveland, 6–1; there's no record of the losing players blaming the loss on the partisan ump. Cantillon never got anywhere near Burns Park, and a riot was averted.

Charley O'Leary, Tiger shortstop during the pennant-winning years of 1907–9, began his career with the White Sox. He recalled a game when he and his Chicago teammates faced the wrath of Burns Park's violent denizens.

"We won by one run and as we left the park the crowd came at us with beer bottles," O'Leary said, according to the *Detroit Free Press*. "It was the bottom of the bus for everybody, and as I was the most scared, I got there first, I guess. Anyway, everybody else piled on top of me, and we rode into town that way. I was nearly smothered. They had a hard time inducing me to believe that that was not an everyday occurrence."

Longtime Tiger owner Walter O. Briggs nostalgically remembered the Burns Park rowdyism: "Those were the days! Why, you used to see more fights on a Sunday afternoon than you now see in the big leagues in five years," Briggs said, according to a *Free Press* article. "The players fought each other and the fans; the fans fought the gate tenders; and the tenders fought the ground keeper. The customers would come all ginned up; fights started because a ball was pitched, lasted throughout the game, and continued long afterward."

The fisticuffs often continued after games in the bar at Garvey's Stockyard Hotel across the street from the Sunday ballpark.

Detroit police guard the field during the 1936 home opener at Navin Field.

"Most Burns Park contests were decided at the bar," the *Detroit News* observed.

Under pressure from league president Johnson, Burns sold the Tigers in 1902, and the team stopped playing at Burns Park, although the battle over Sunday baseball was far from finished.

THE TIGERS FOUND THEMSELVES in their first pennant race in 1907, and baseball fever engulfed Detroit. Elected officials jumped on the bandwagon and started heavily agitating for Sunday ball at Michigan and Trumbull. Although it was widely reported that most Detroiters favored relaxing the blue laws, the vocal, powerful ministers' lobby wouldn't budge.

In February, State Representative George Duncan introduced a bill to legalize Sunday baseball in Michigan. The bill fizzled amid fierce opposition from the religious group. Two months later, State Representative George G. Scott floated a proposal to change the city charter to allow Sunday ball. The suggestion likewise went nowhere.

As the season played out, with the Tigers battling the Philadelphia A's for the American League pennant, Police Commissioner Fred Smith publicly declared he would look the other way if the Tigers played Sunday ball in the city limits. The city's top cop announcing he would ignore blatant violations of the law rankled the prohibitionists, but Smith stood firm.

The first Sunday game at Bennett Park was on August 18, 1907, against the New York Highlanders before an overflow crowd of 9,635 fans. The Tigers trounced the New Yorkers, 13–6, and the *Free Press* proclaimed in its front-page headline the next day: "No Incident Mars Sunday Ball Game."

In an attempt to ease ruffled feathers, the Tigers announced they were donating $200 of the gate receipts to Detroit's Protestant and Roman Catholic orphan asylums. It didn't work. The Reverend John Sweet of Simpson Methodist Church, head of the Detroit Pastor's Union, expressed outrage after the game.

"The responsibility for this lawlessness rests with the police department," Sweet told the *News*. "They were notified of the [plan to play Sunday ball at Bennett Park]…yet the police did nothing. They refused to interfere, and this dreadful crime was committed within 100 feet of a police station, and while police officers looked on, making themselves parties to the crime."

The "dreadful crime" would be repeated two more times that season with no reported incidents.

In June 1908, Wayne County prosecutor George B. Yerkes, under continued pressure from the Pastor's Union, asked the police commissioner to stop the Tigers from playing Sunday ball at Bennett Park, in accordance with the laws on the books. Smith rebuffed the prosecutor's request, prompting the Pastor's Union to seek a writ of mandamus compelling the police commissioner to uphold the law. Wayne County circuit judges ruled that they had no jurisdiction over the matter. The decision was appealed, and in July 1908, the Michigan Supreme Court declined to hear the case, effectively denuding the Pastor's Union's attempts to legally block Sunday baseball in Detroit, although it would continue railing against it.

It was a losing battle. Detroit's rooters—and the media—clearly wanted the Tigers to continue ignoring the city's blue laws. The team owners obliged (and enjoyed fat gate receipts from lusty Sunday crowds).

"The whole issue is that those opposed to Sunday baseball have tried to make a moral issue out of it," the *Detroit Journal* opined in 1908. "They have conceived and contended that Sunday baseball is a sin, which per se it is not. Sunday is the one day in seven on which thousands of workingmen and boys can attend public baseball games. Bennett Park for boys and men is a better and safer place than suburban saloons and road houses."

Although blue laws in some form would remain on the books in Michigan until the twenty-first century, Sunday baseball in Detroit became a permanent, vital part of the schedule following the 1908 state supreme court ruling.

Philadelphia was the major league's last holdout, with the Phillies and Athletics finally lifting the Sunday baseball ban in 1934.

Ty Cobb and Billy Martin probably hold the crowns in their respective divisions as the most combative player and manager to ever don the Olde English *D*—but Cobb wasn't the first Tiger player to jump into the stands to go after a fan, nor was Martin the first Tiger manager to get into drunken brawls. Both men were merely carrying on a Tiger tradition almost as old as the team itself.

The Tigers had been a major-league club for only seventeen days when, on May 11, 1901, manager George Stallings reportedly left a game to beat up a man named Walter Barber, who was handing out scorecards outside the ballpark.

"Barber claims that he was distributing a free score card outside of Bennett Park during the course of a game and was assaulted by Stallings," the *News* reported. "He claims to have been very roughly handled."

Barber filed a lawsuit seeking $2,000 in damages, although it was unclear what had sparked the alleged violence. The case wound its way through the court system for two years until it was thrown out because Barber didn't show up to court. Whether Stallings was guilty or not, he could be an ornery cuss; while managing Buffalo in the Eastern League, he was arrested for fighting with a Providence police officer.

The mayhem at Bennett Park continued on May 26, 1901, when an umpire climbed into the stands and chased a fan during a game against the Washington Nationals.

The *Free Press* noted that umpire Jack Sheridan, who worked as an undertaker in the off-season, "invited a riot by jumping over the fence along the left field foul line, after a spectator who threw a ball out on the field which accidentally struck [Washington first baseman–catcher Mike] Grandy.

"Sheridan evidentially wanted to make a grandstand play, claiming that the person who threw the ball did it intentionally to harm the visiting catcher," the *Free Press* said. "Even had this been true, Sheridan's attack on the spectator was uncalled for. The duty of the umpire is to try to cut out all rowdyism on the ballfield, but instead of doing this, Sheridan seems to be trying to act the part of a rowdy himself."

A year later, on June 20, 1902, it was Tiger right fielder James "Ducky" Holmes's turn to hop into the stands and go after a fan. It happened during the fourth inning of a game against the Boston Pilgrims. Holmes was having a rough day, "having been caught trying to steal in the [first inning], and having been struck out in the third, with two men on bases," the *Free Press* reported.

"An occupant of the right field bleachers called Holmes a vile name when he came close to the stand on a play," the *Free Press* said. "Holmes lost his temper and climbed into the bleachers to attack the fellow. Other players reached him in time to prevent a conflict. Two policemen found the man who started the bother and ejected him from the grounds. Another person who had taken part in the talk hid under the bleachers and lost himself in a crowd."

Violence and controversy were firmly established during the early years of the Detroit Tigers—and Ty Cobb hadn't even joined the team yet.

2
PSYCHO IN SPIKES

Tyrus Raymond Cobb's life was a ball of fire and chaos before he ever stepped foot in Detroit.

He was a mixture of intelligence, hypersensitivity and unhinged rage. The personality emerged early. Cobb said he beat up a classmate in the fifth grade who caused the boys to lose to the girls in the school spelling bee.

"I had a terrible temper in my younger days, and it got me into a lot of trouble," he wrote in a 1914 syndicated newspaper memoir.

Trouble there was, although Cobb's status as one of the most famous men in the United States helped him wiggle out of most of the jams he caused. In the long run, though, his reputation didn't get off so easy.

He was born on December 18, 1886, in rural Royston, Georgia. His father was a state senator, school superintendent and newspaper editor, while his mother came from a family of well-to-do landowners.

The baseball bug bit young Tyrus early on, and as he grew into his teens, his hankering for the diamond was a constant source of tension with his father. William Herschel Cobb was dead set against his eldest son choosing a profession that was thought of at the time as being only one step above bank robber. Cobb worshiped his father and wanted to please him—but he wanted to play ball even more.

When the seventeen-year-old Cobb was offered a tryout by the Augusta Tourists in the South Atlantic League in 1904, his father finally relented and gave his grudging consent for the boy to get it out of his system. He hoped his son would eventually quit baseball, go to college and get a real job.

Ty Cobb arrived in Detroit in 1905 with controversy swirling around him after his mother fatally shot his father. There were rumors she was having an affair and that her husband was sneaking home to check on her, when she shot him with a pistol. Following a high-profile trial, she was acquitted of murder charges.

The tryout went well, and Cobb's professional career was under way. While he was known during his two years in the minor leagues for his wild, sometimes reckless playing style, there are no recorded incidents of the violent episodes that would mark his time in the majors.

During his second season as a pro, Cobb tore up the South Atlantic "Sally" League. He was on his way toward winning his first batting championship, and rumors about a possible sale to a big-league club were circulating when, on August 8, 1905, Cobb's world was blown to smithereens.

Imagine the horror of opening a telegram and reading something along the lines of "COME HOME IMMEDIATELY STOP YOUR MOTHER SHOT YOUR FATHER DEAD STOP."

On the fatal morning, W.H. Cobb had told his wife he was taking a road trip for a few days to visit schools he supervised in the district. That night, he hitched his wagon and shoved off—but he circled back and returned home. Rumor had it that the mister was trying to catch the missus, Amanda Cobb, with her lover.

Whatever the reason for his return, the man known around town as "Professor Cobb" was lurking near his house when, at about 11:00 p.m., his wife said she heard a rustling sound outside her bedroom window.

"Thinking the man was a robber, she seized [a] pistol from under her pillow and fired twice," the *Washington Post* reported days after the incident. "The man fell, and then, she says, she learned she had killed her husband."

W.H. Cobb died from two gunshot wounds to the abdomen. His wife was arrested at the funeral while she stood over the open grave and charged with voluntary manslaughter. Bail was set at $7,000.

The case drew national interest, fueled by the rumors of Amanda Cobb's infidelity.

"It developed to-day…that Cobb had been warned to watch his home," the *Washington Post* reported. "The senator left town, ostensibly to go to Atlanta, but returned at night to watch. There was a male visitor and the killing of the husband followed. This is the theory of the State, but the name of the visitor to Senator Cobb's home has not been divulged. Mrs. Cobb is a very beautiful woman, and there has been gossip about her for some time."

Three weeks after the incident, the Detroit Tigers purchased Cobb's contract from Augusta for $700. His dream had come true, but his beloved father wasn't there to see it.

Cobb reported to Detroit with storm clouds swirling around him.

COBB'S ARRIVAL IN THE big city was met with little fanfare. He was considered a stopgap fill-in outfielder after the Tigers were hit by a slew of injuries.

"If he gets away with a .275 mark, he will be satisfying everybody," the *Detroit Free Press* famously prophesized.

On August 30, 1905, Cobb made his major-league debut against the New York Highlanders, socking a double off future Hall of Fame pitcher Jack Chesbro in his first at bat. Cobb got into forty-one games that year, hitting an unremarkable .240, although even with his family tragedy hanging over him, he showed flashes of his future greatness.

The following season, the trouble that would mark Cobb's tumultuous career began. His teammates, who had basically ignored him during the previous year's stint, began brutally hazing him in the 1906 spring training camp. It was common to razz young players in those days, but the Tigers were particularly cruel to Cobb. They sawed his bats in two, flattened his hats, threw wet newspapers at his head during train trips and locked him out of the shower after games. On top of that, the team's burly catcher repeatedly beat him up.

Longtime *Detroit Free Press* baseball writer E.A. Batchelor wrote that Cobb's teammates were jealous of the highbrowed rookie. While the other Tigers

A *Detroit News* photographer snapped a photo during Cobb's first major-league game on August 30, 1905, as the outfielder talks with Tiger manager Bill Armour.

spent their time after road games getting hammered in bars or watching tawdry vaudeville shows, Cobb toured museums and libraries.

"That Ty came from a higher social plane than had spawned the bullies made them all the more determined to drive him off the squad," Batchelor wrote.

Tiger catcher Charlie "Boss" Schmidt, a former professional wrestler who according to legend used his bare fists to drive spikes into the Tiger clubhouse's wood floor, fought with Cobb twice that year. Schmidt reportedly whipped the younger man both times. There would be more vicious fights between the two the following season, with Cobb on the losing end.

Between the bullying and his mother's manslaughter charges, Cobb must have been under tremendous pressure. Toward the end of spring training, he left the team to attend his mother's trial, which lasted only two days. On March 30, 1906, the jury deliberated just an hour before finding Amanda Cobb not guilty.

Once the season began, it became clear that Cobb was one of baseball's rising stars, which seemed to fuel his teammates' resentment. In July, it all seemed to come to a head when Cobb left the team. Tiger officials told reporters that their young outfielder had gone to the hospital for an unspecified operation, although baseball historians generally conclude that Cobb's forty-four-day absence likely was spent in a sanatorium recovering from a nervous breakdown.

Cobb returned to the Tigers in September. A few weeks later, he got into a dustup with a fellow Tiger in St. Louis. Cobb's teammates were upset because he and outfielder Matty McIntyre, who despised the Georgian, had allowed a ball to fall between them during a game against the Browns. Tiger pitcher Eddie Siever, McIntyre's close friend, blamed Cobb for the misplay.

Later, in the Planters' Hotel, Cobb tangled with Siever and tore him to pieces.

"Cobb was standing in the lobby, leaning against one of the columns… when Siever passed and, it is said, called him an ugly name," the *Free Press* reported. "Quick as a flash, Cobb sent out his right fist, catching Siever under the chin and flooring him. Cobb followed the blow with several others, and kicked Siever in the face after he had fallen to the floor.

"Other players finally separated the combatants, after Siever's face was a mass of bruises," the *Free Press* said. "Cobb walked calmly out of the hotel, and physicians were called to care for the wounded pitcher. No arrests were made, as the team left St. Louis a short time after the fight."

The fight resulted in "severe disfigurement of Siever's face," the *Free Press* reported. "Cobb was not scratched."

Despite all the distractions, Cobb ended his first full season with a solid .316 batting average, good for sixth in the American League.

COBB'S MENACING SIDE EMERGED in 1907, during one of the most combative spring training camps in baseball history.

During the first week of training in Augusta's Warren Park, as Cobb walked to afternoon practice, he assaulted Henry "Bungy" Cummings, the ballpark's twenty-five-year-old groundskeeper, who was black—a fact played up by the *Free Press*, which started as a proslavery paper and was overtly racist well into the twentieth century.

"The negro stepped up to the Georgia boy, held out his hand, and said 'Hello, Ty, old boy,'" the *Free Press* reported the day after the March 16, 1907 incident. "Being a southerner, Cobb considered the action of the negro in putting himself on an equal footing with a white man, an insult. He drew

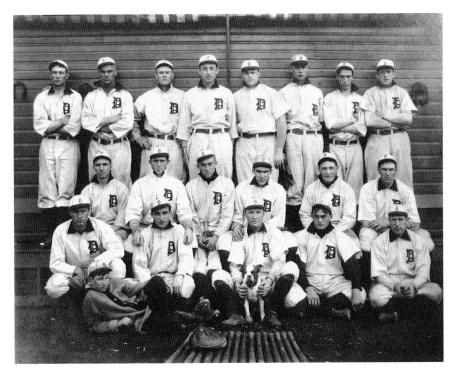

Cobb's body language in this team photo, taken during spring training 1907, one of the most volatile training camps in baseball history, speaks volumes, as Cobb (*middle row, third from left*) feuded with most of his teammates.

back the hand that the negro had reached out for and, instead of extending it for a handshake, drove it forward, hitting the man with a hard blow. He chased the negro off the playing lot and into the club house."

Schmidt, who already had attacked Cobb at least twice, told reporters that Cobb had also tried to strangle the groundskeeper's wife. "[Cummings's wife] went to the rescue of the man, applying an epithet to Cobb," the *Free Press* said. "The latter at once turned his attention to the woman, grabbing her and choking her."

Cobb disputed the allegation, and none of Detroit's other newspapers mentioned Bungy's wife being assaulted.

According to all accounts of the incident, Schmidt jumped on Cobb, and the two men scuffled before teammates broke it up.

The assault is often used as an example of Cobb's racism, but the newspapers—chiefly, the *Free Press*—made a bigger deal out of Cummings's skin color than Cobb did. For all his faults, Cobb's extensive, well-documented record shows no evidence of racial bigotry, other than what appear to be a few contemporary columnists' uncorroborated flights of fancy. But that reputation stuck for years, with well-respected historians repeating falsehoods as fact until researchers recently pored over the record and debunked most of the anecdotes about Cobb's supposed racial bigotry.

Cobb likely didn't learn to be a racist from his father, who, as a politician in the antebellum Deep South, openly advocated for African Americans' rights and once stopped a lynching by standing up to a riotous crowd. During the younger Cobb's baseball career, he often visited Negro League games and hung out with black ballplayers. After Jackie Robinson broke the color line in 1947, Cobb praised black players joining the big leagues, at a time when many in baseball circles openly opposed it. When Cobb died, at least one African American newspaper lauded him for endorsing blacks in the majors. A black employee named his son after Cobb.

If Cobb was as racist as he's been made out to be, there's no record of him ever revealing it in hundreds of interviews, even though during his era he could have done so with no repercussions. Tris Speaker, probably

Alexander George Washington Rivers was a black employee of Cobb's for eighteen years and named his firstborn Ty Cobb Rivers. In addition to Cobb's well-deserved reputation as a man with a hair-trigger temper, many called him a racist, although recent research suggests that claim is erroneous.

While Cobb was among the most cantankerous players in baseball history, he also had a soft side.

the AL's second-best player during Cobb's era, was an openly racist KKK member and got no flak for it. And although Cobb was never shy about speaking his mind, he was never quoted saying anything but positive things about blacks.

Cobb's first recorded statement on race came in 1952, when he told the *Sporting News*: "The Negro should be accepted wholeheartedly and not grudgingly into baseball. The Negro has the right to play professional sports, and who's to say he has not?"

But whether or not Cobb's Warren Park skirmish with the groundskeeper was racially motivated, it serves as an example of his violent, uncontrollable temper. There were more dustups during the trouble-filled spring training of 1907, including another fight between Cobb and Schmidt in Meridian, Mississippi, as the Tigers barnstormed northward to Detroit. Again, Schmidt soundly thrashed the younger player. The incident made national headlines, and it prompted Tiger management to contemplate trading Cobb to Cleveland straight up for outfielder Elmer Flick, who was winding down his Hall of Fame career.

After the 1907 season started, however, the Tigers would thank the heavens they didn't pull the trigger on that trade, as Cobb quickly established himself as the most exciting player in baseball, and the fighting with teammates ceased.

In the future, most of Tyrus's roiling fury would be unleashed on the rest of the world, not on fellow Tigers.

COBB AND TIGER FIRST baseman Claude Rossman were strolling out of the Pontchartrain Hotel in downtown Detroit on their way to a game at Bennett Park the afternoon of June 6, 1908, when they came upon Fred Collins, a black employee of the Detroit United Railway who was spreading asphalt outside the hotel. According to newspaper reports, Cobb took offense when Collins told him to walk around the wet patch of sidewalk, so Cobb handled the dispute like he often did—by hauling off and punching the man.

The *Free Press* again made race a central issue, with cringeworthy coverage of the fight.

The headline quipped: "Cobb Increases His Batting Average by Battering Up a Negro Wearing Spectacles." A cartoon accompanying the story depicts an ape-like figure with absurdly huge lips fighting with Cobb, while three similar dark caricatures wielding rakes and hoes rush to join in. The next panel shows a cop gripping both men by the shoulders, looking at their blackened faces and asking: "Which one of youse is Ty Cobb?"

The *Free Press* story told how Cobb became belligerent when Collins told another man he couldn't walk on the freshly poured asphalt.

"Cobb evidently thought that Collins spoke to him, and turned sharply on the negro, demanding: 'What the - - - have you got to say about it, nigger?' The negro evidently didn't treat Cobb with the deference the colored brother extends to the white man down in dear old Georgia and Cobb was seen to shove his face within two inches of the shiny continence of the Ethiopian.

"Half way through the fight, as Cobb was driving the negro towards the curb, five burly negroes, fellow-workers of Collins, advanced toward the fighters with upraised ironers, weighing 75 pounds each, and a sixth negro flourished a rake," the *Free Press* reported. "The two struggling men were whirling and fighting so fast that the negroes did not get a chance to let the deadly weapons down on Cobb's head. They evidently feared they might hit the negro by mistake.

"Just as the negroes' weapons seemed sure to fall, white men rushed to the assistance of Cobb," the *Free Press* said. "They grabbed the big iron bludgeons and rake, and pushed the negroes back."

Did the *Free Press* quote Cobb accurately? Did he hurl that racial slur at Collins? Did the *Free Press* reporter witness the fight, or did he invent details, as was common in those days? Definitive answers are lost to history, although coverage of the fight by the *Detroit News* and the *Detroit Times* doesn't mention a racial element, other than the fact that Collins was a "Negro."

Independent of any racial animus, Cobb did assault the man, and the ballplayer was issued a summons to appear in municipal court the next day. Police court justice Edward J. Jeffries Sr., whose son Edward Jr. would serve as Detroit mayor in the 1940s, said Cobb's status as a ballplayer cut no ice with him.

"If you are guilty you will pay a fine," Jeffries told Cobb. "Your batting average won't save you." The judge set a court date for the following week, but before the hearing could take place, Cobb settled with Collins for seventy-five dollars.

Cobb later told reporters: "When a man is insulted it is worth $75 to get satisfaction. I would have done the same thing to any man."

If Cobb felt insulted by a black man giving him orders, as the *Free Press* claimed, no newspaper ever quoted him as such. Conversely, his statement "I would have done the same thing to any man" suggests that perhaps race didn't play a role in the skirmish.

Cobb could be a dangerous man with a hair-trigger temper, and the record shows he'd fight anyone, black or white, at the drop of a hat.

THE YEAR 1909 SAW yet more controversy for Cobb. On August 24, in a game against the Philadelphia Athletics, Cobb slid hard into third base, scraping third baseman Frank "Home Run" Baker with his spikes. Philly fans were outraged, and Cobb received numerous death threats. Philadelphia police took the threats seriously, stationing officers throughout the stands when the Tigers next visited the City of Brotherly Love. The closest thing to an incident was when a car outside Shibe Park backfired. Cobb, mistaking the sound for a gunshot, reportedly jumped several inches into the air.

On September 3, 1909, Cobb took his fury to a new level, stabbing a man during a skirmish in a Cleveland hotel.

The Tigers were in town for a three-game series and staying at the Euclid Hotel. The day's game had been called on account of darkness in the ninth inning of a 1–1 tie. Afterward, Cobb took in the new George M. Cohen musical *The Man Who Owns Broadway* at the Euclid Avenue Opera House.

There are varying reports about what happened when Cobb returned to the hotel at about 2:15 a.m. The hotel manager said Cobb was drunk and couldn't find his room, while Cobb claimed he hadn't been drinking. According to another story, Cobb wanted to get into a card game in one of the players' rooms, and the bellhop wouldn't let him go to that floor. Either way, there were words with the bellhop, and Cobb reportedly slapped the young man. Things escalated from there.

The play in which Cobb spiked Philadelphia A's third baseman Frank "Home Run" Baker in 1909—one of several controversies Cobb found himself in during his twenty-four-year career. After the incident, Cobb needed police protection when he played in Philadelphia's Shibe Park.

"When I came to the elevator, where the trouble started, I found that Cobb had struck the elevator boy," George Stanfield, the hotel's night watchman, told the *Free Press*.

> *He began calling me vile names. I struck him. We sparred, and then my foot slipped and I fell, striking my head against the elevator grating. Cobb was on me in an instant, saying, "I'll kill you now." I felt the sting of a knife. The blood welled up under my collar from a deep cut on my shoulder. It dripped down into my eyes from a gash in the scalp. Through the blood I saw his hand descending to my face, and I threw up my left hand to shield my face. The knife blade passed clear through it. I threw him off and started backing away, flourishing a gun. I seized my club from the hotel desk and struck a blow that brought him to his knees. I struck him again and he raised his hands above his head and begged me not to kill him.*

Cobb gave a different version of events. "The watchman became insulting and I protested that I never deserved the treatment I was being accorded," he told the *Chicago Tribune*.

> *The watchman made threats....[A]s I stepped toward the elevator the watchman struck me in the head from behind. Then I turned around and sailed into him. I had him down on the floor and was punching him when he sunk his fingernails into my eyelids....I pulled out a knife and slashed it across his hand. Then he released his hold. As he backed toward the grill room entrance, he drew a gun and covered me. Holding the gun in one hand, he walked up and struck me several times with his billy [club]. He asked the clerk who I was and the clerk said he didn't know. Then I went to my room.*

In the ball game hours later, Cobb, who seemed to thrive amid controversy, went 3 for 4. Meanwhile, as Cobb cavorted around the baseball diamond, hotel management was at Cleveland police headquarters pressing charges.

Two days after the stabbing, a Cleveland grand jury indicted Cobb for assault with intent to murder, and Stanfield told reporters he was suing the ballplayer for $5,000.

An arrest warrant was issued for Cobb, who slipped out of League Park to evade police.

"The Detroit team had got wind of the fact that a warrant had been issued for Ty's arrest, and they hurried and scurried about so that the breaker of the peace and quietude of the Hotel Euclid could escape the clutches of the law," the Associated Press reported. Tiger manager Hughie Jennings then whisked Cobb away in a sedan, according to the story.

On September 8, a Cleveland police detective traveled to Detroit to serve Cobb with the warrant. Stanfield had agreed to drop the charges and lawsuit in exchange for a $115 payoff, but Cleveland prosecutors forged ahead with the case without their star witness.

Cobb probably wasn't in a good mood when he was indicted on October 20. Only four days earlier, his Tigers had lost their third straight World Series to the Pittsburgh Pirates in the first Fall Classic to go the full seven games. Cobb pleaded not guilty and posted a $500 bond. A November 22 trial date was set.

Without the victim's cooperation, prosecutors didn't have much of a case. After a hearing in which Cobb reportedly whipped out the knife that he'd used in the fight and showed it to the judge, the ballplayer was fined $100.

Cobb patted his pockets and told the judge he didn't have the cash on him but that he'd make good on it the next time the Tigers were in Cleveland. The judge let the superstar ballplayer slide.

For about a quarter of the price of one of Henry Ford's new contraptions, the Model T, Cobb was able to pay off his victim, pay a fine and avoid going to prison.

COBB WASN'T THE FIRST baseball player to assault a fan in the stands, nor was he the last. But his rage on May 15, 1912, in New York has probably garnered more discussion through the years than all the other incidents combined.

The Tigers were playing the final game of a four-game series in Hilltop Park against the New York Highlanders, who were sometimes called the Yankees. Throughout the series, a fan named Claude Lucker had heckled Cobb relentlessly. In the final game of the series, Lucker ramped up the verbal barrage, bellowing at Cobb from his seat in the third row along the third-base line.

Cobb stayed in the field during the top of the third inning so he wouldn't have to pass the abusive fan. Finally, in the fourth inning, as he jogged to his position, Cobb took a right turn, jumped over the railing into the stands and began pummeling Lucker, a former pressman who was missing one hand and three fingers from his other hand, the result of an accident with a *New York Times* printing press.

The day after the assault, newspapers across the country joked about it.

"It long has been a recognized fact that Ty Cobb is a great hitter, but until this afternoon it was not known that his hitting ability extended beyond the batter's box," *Free Press* reporter E.A. Batchelor wrote. "It does, however, as the fan who received his attentions will testify. In the excitement, an accurate count was impossible, of course, but it was the general opinion among the scorers that Ty had a perfect average in his hitting against the spectator's map."

The *New York Evening World* headline read: "Cobb of Tigers Hits Effectively, but with His Fist This Time."

Even the usually staid *New York Times* was gleeful. "Everything was very pleasant...until Ty Cobb johnnykilbaned a spectator right on the place where he talks, started the claret, and stopped the flow of profane and vulgar words," the *Times* reported, dropping a reference to Johnny Kilbane, a featherweight boxer of the day. "Cobb led with a left jab and countered with a right kick to Mr. Spectator's left [eye], which made his peeper look as if someone had drawn a curtain over it....Ty used a change of pace and had nice control. Jabs bounded off the spectator's face like a golf ball from a rock."

Lucker gave the *Times* his less mirthful side of the story:

> Cobb vaulted over the fence where I was sitting in the third row and made straight for me. He struck me with his fists on the forehead over the left eye, and knocked me down. Then he jumped on me and spiked me in the left leg and kicked me in the side, after which he booted me behind the left ear. I was down and Cobb was kicking me when someone in the crowd shouted, "Don't kick him, he has no hands." Cobb answered, "I don't care if he has no feet!"

Cobb shrugged off the incident to the *Detroit News*: "Everybody took it as a joke. I was only kidding that fellow, and I frightened him to death, but I would not take from the United States Army what that man said to me and the fans in New York cheered me to the echo when I left the field. I don't look for applause, but for the first time in my life, I was glad the fans were with me."

Most of the New York writers seemed to sympathize with Cobb.

"Spectators in the vicinity said the man had been giving Cobb a verbal grilling for some time, that he had been warned to keep still, and that his language was decidedly personal and offensive," the *New York Sun* said.

The *New York Tribune* blamed Highlander ownership. "American League Park, New York, is rapidly earning an odious reputation," the paper said. "While one of [team owner] Frank Farrell's grim-faced Pinkertons stood idly within earshot, a noisy 'fan' in the left field stands, at yesterday's game, heaped abuse and vilification on Ty Cobb until the outraged player was provoked into administering a well-deserved beating....When Cobb walked off the field the few hisses that greeted him were drowned in vigorous applause."

American League president Ban Johnson, who was in the stands that day, wasn't as amused as the sportswriters seemed to be.

"There is no provocation sufficient to make a player in this league so far forget himself as to leave the playing field, rush into the stands, and assault a spectator," Johnson said.

Newspaper accounts suggest Lucker was talked out of pressing charges against Cobb, although that didn't faze the league president, who suspended Cobb indefinitely.

Cobb's teammates were so upset by the suspension that they staged the first player strike in baseball history, announcing they wouldn't play the upcoming May 18 game against the Philadelphia Athletics. League president Ban Johnson told Tiger owner Frank Navin he'd fine him $5,000 if the Tigers forfeited the game, so Navin ordered manager Hughie Jennings to find any warm bodies he could so a team could be fielded.

Jennings complied, cobbling together a squad of amateur and semipro ballplayers who were willing to be humiliated by the two-time defending world champion A's. The players were paid twenty-five dollars each, although pitcher Allan Travers was paid fifty dollars. Jennings also pressed two coaches into service: Joe Sugden, forty-one, and Deacon McGuire, forty-eight.

As expected, the A's destroyed the ragtag aggregation, 24–2.

Following the farce, Cobb begged his teammates to end the walkout, and they did. Ban Johnson fined the striking players $100 each—double Cobb's fine of $50—although he also incurred a ten-day suspension for the assault on Lucker.

THE RECORD SHOWS THAT Cobb didn't need an excuse to fight—and he surely wasn't one to refuse an invitation. On March 31, 1917, New York Giants second baseman Charles "Buck" Herzog challenged Cobb and lived to regret it.

The Tigers were training in Waxahachie, Texas, for the second spring in a row, after previously setting up spring camp in places like San Antonio and Augusta. In late March, the team broke camp and headed north, stopping in Fort Worth and then in Dallas to play a series of exhibitions against the New York Giants, who would eventually win the National League pennant that year before losing to the Chicago White Sox in the World Series.

Cobb had played eighteen holes of golf at the River Crest Country Club in Fort Worth the morning of March 31 and arrived late to Gardner Park. Giant players Art Fletcher and Herzog razzed Cobb for his lateness, calling him a "southern swellhead" and "showoff," according to newspaper reports.

With two outs in the third inning, Cobb rapped a single and hollered to Herzog that he planned to steal second on the next pitch. Cobb did just that, and although the throw from catcher Lew McCarty beat him easily, the Georgia Peach slid hard into the second sacker.

"Cobb spiked Herzog, cutting a long gash in the latter's left leg," the *Austin American-Statesman* reported. "The players started fighting at once, with Cobb on top of Herzog, and Fletcher on top of Cobb, and players from both sides participating in a battle royal."

Umpire Bill Brennan threw Cobb out of the game, angering the five thousand fans who had come to see the game's biggest star. Dallas-area newspaper advertisements leading up to the series had promised "Ty Cobb will play."

"It was necessary to call in the police reserve so that the game could be completed without a general riot," the *Detroit News* said.

The game continued, and the Giants won, 5–3. Afterward, the players went to the Oriental Hotel, where both teams were staying.

While Cobb was eating dinner in the hotel dining room, Herzog, who had done some boxing in the army, reportedly challenged Cobb to meet him at 8:00 p.m. in Cobb's hotel room. Of course, Cobb agreed.

Fight time was still an hour away, giving Cobb time to head up to room 404 and move the furniture out of the way. Always looking for an edge, Cobb claimed he sprinkled water on the floor and put on street shoes with leather soles for a better grip. He said he guessed Zimmerman would wear gym shoes, which wouldn't get good traction on the wet floor.

Several players and reporters jammed the fourth-floor corridor outside the room. Cobb and Herzog laid out the ground rules for their fight: Each combatant could have someone from his team in the room with him; the Giants chose third baseman Heinie Zimmerman, and the Tigers picked catcher Oscar Stanage. It was further agreed to allow Tiger trainer Harry Tuthill to referee the bout.

Then, the men stripped to the waist and went at it.

According to legend, Herzog did show up wearing sneakers, which caused him to slip on the watery floor, negating his superior boxing skills. By all accounts, Cobb whipped the daylights out of him.

"A few short jabs were exchanged, and Herzog went to the floor," the *Corsicana Daily Sun* reported. "Cobb waited until he arose and swung a wicked right to Herzog's eye, cutting a small gash just above the eye. Several blows were exchanged, neither gaining until Cobb sent three or four blows to Herzog's face, causing the blood to flow from his nose."

The *Detroit Free Press* reported: "They fought probably five minutes until Herzog announced that he had had enough and shook hands with his conqueror. During the battle, 'Buck' was somewhat cut up around the face, while Ty did not have a mark."

"The scrap this evening was one that Cobb could not have avoided without being charged with cowardice, for Herzog threw down the gauntlet and would not have been satisfied without the encounter," the *Free Press* said. "It is possible that the bad blood thus far manifested between the two teams will not be so much in evidence now that there has been a good fight."

But the bad blood continued. Cobb refused to play the Giants for the rest of their exhibition tour; instead, he went to Cincinnati and continued spring training with the Reds. After the Tigers and Giants finished their series of games in Kansas City, the Giants reportedly sent a taunting telegram to Cobb: "It's safe to rejoin your club now. We've left."

COBB'S FURY ON THE diamond continued until his retirement in 1928, although his off-field violence abated after World War I, in which he served as a captain in a poison gas unit.

Although he'd mellowed a bit after the "War to End all Wars," his old anger resurfaced from time to time. On September 24, 1921, Cobb had one of his most vicious fights, a knockdown, drag-out with Billy Evans, the American League's chief umpire, in front of about fifty fans. According to reports, Cobb won.

The animosity was sparked in the fifth inning, when Evans called Cobb out on an attempted steal of second base. Cobb—by now managing the Tigers—got in the umpire's face, threatening to beat him up right on the field. Cooler heads prevailed, and the game continued. But after the Tigers' 5–1 loss to the Senators, as Cobb and Evans passed each other on the way to their respective locker rooms, they went at it, while dozens of fans looked on.

The *News* gave a blow-by-blow description: "Evans suffered a cut lip where Cobb's mighty fist landed, and his neck was cut from cinders in which both men rolled before the eyes of a half a hundred delighted fans. Clinching, they went to the cinders and were rolling around when park officials succeeded in separating them. It was officially announced afterwards that they shook hands and agreed to call it quits."

Both combatants reportedly agreed not to tell league officials about the fight—a meaningless pact, since the incident had been witnessed by so many fans and was covered by newspapers across the country. Johnson suspended Cobb for one game. Evans umpired the next few games wearing bandages.

If Ty Cobb played today, he likely wouldn't get away with half the things he did, although there certainly are modern examples of sports stars getting free passes for abhorrent behavior.

Cobb's legacy is violence, although there's much more to the story. He gave generously to charity, building a hospital in his native Royston, Georgia, and setting up a scholarship for medical students. Cobb, a sharp stock market manipulator who invested heavily in budding stocks like Coca-Cola and General Motors, was known to quietly give money to old ballplayers who'd fallen on hard times.

There are a lot of false rumors about Cobb, but his story doesn't need embellishing. It's fascinating enough as is.

3

THE FIX IS IN?

Gamblers have been a part of baseball from the beginning. The sport's first major betting scandal erupted in 1865, when New York Mutuals catcher William Wansley took $100 from gamblers to throw a September game against the Brooklyn Eckfords. Wansley gave $30 each to Mutuals shortstop Tom Devyr and third baseman Ed Duffy to help toss the game. They got the job done, as the Brooklyn team steamrolled the Mutuals, 23–11.

An early gambling controversy that rocked baseball involved Detroit's National League team, the Wolverines. It remains one of the few times in baseball history when an umpire was found to have been crooked.

The dirty ump was Dick Higham, a former player who had hit into the first triple play in National League history in 1876. Despite Higham's reputation as a shady character, the National League hired him as an umpire in 1881. The decision proved to be as dumb as it seemed when they first did it.

During baseball's early days, umpires often stayed with one team for extended periods, to save on traveling costs. Higham worked twenty-six of the Wolverines' first twenty-nine games of the 1882 season, and Detroit mayor and team owner William G. Thompson became suspicious when the ump ruled against the Detroit squad on almost every close play during those games.

Thompson hired detectives to investigate. The Pinkertons intercepted a letter from Higham to gambler James Todd that showed the two men were in cahoots. Higham wrote: "If I want you to [bet on] the Detroits

Wednesday, I will telegraph you in this way, 'Buy all the lumber you can.' If you don't hear from me, don't [bet on] the Detroits."

The Wolverine owner brought up the matter with league officials, who ignored the offense of tampering with the U.S. Mail and focused on the umpire.

"Higham denied the authorship of the letter, but other letters of his were produced and the signature 'Dick' was declared by three bank experts to be the same," the *Detroit News* reported. "This prompt action on the part of the Detroit association clears their skirts of any insinuation of crookedness."

The National League board issued its ruling that "Richard Higham be forever disqualified from acting as an umpire in any game of ball participated in by a league club."

THE BOOKMAKING SCOURGE LIKELY played a part in an early Tiger tragedy, when, in 1903, newly appointed manager George "Win" Mercer committed suicide and reportedly left a note warning against the evils of gambling.

Mercer had a nine-year playing career as a pitcher with some pop in his bat. He joined the Tigers in 1902 and had one of his best years, posting a career-best 3.02 earned run average while notching a 15-18 won-loss record. He pitched twenty-eight complete games and threw four shutouts, good enough for second in the league.

Mercer also served as a recruiter for the Tigers. After the American League declared itself a major league in 1901, National League players began jumping their contracts for better offers from teams in the new circuit. In August 1902, Mercer was dispatched to Cincinnati, where he wooed future Hall-of-Famer "Wahoo" Sam Crawford. Crawford would join the Tigers the following year and stay until his retirement in 1917.

At the end of the 1902 season, Mercer was named the Tigers' player-manager. All seemed to be going well. Mercer embarked on a western barnstorming tour with an "All American Team" and, according to newspaper reports, was planning to meet with Tiger management about personnel issues. His teammates on the barnstorming trip, who were in proximity to him as they traveled from town to town, said he acted normally.

But things weren't as they seemed. On January 12, 1903, Mercer checked into the Occidental Hotel in San Francisco, signed the register as George Murray from Philadelphia and killed himself.

"He was assigned a room and must have at once prepared for death," the *Detroit Free Press* reported. "He attached a rubber tubing to the gas burner, and passed the free end to his lips as he lay on the bed, inhaling the fumes.

He had undressed first, and threw his coat and vest over his face to force the gas into his nose and mouth when he should become semi-conscious and release his grip on the tube."

Several letters were found in Mercer's room. One was written to his mother and the other to a "young woman of Washington D.C.," the *Free Press* reported.

A third letter was addressed to James "Tip" O'Neill, who had been a star outfielder in the 1880s and who'd helped Mercer organize the barnstorming tour.

"A word to my boy friends," Mercer wrote. "Beware of women and a game of chance. Well, dear old pal, with tears in my eyes, I say good-bye forever. May everyone connected to our trip forgive me. I wanted to do right. Please forgive me, old pal."

PRIOR TO THE 1919 Black Sox scandal, in which eight Chicago players agreed to throw the World Series to the Cincinnati Reds, rumors of Fall Classic fixes were commonplace. In two of the Tigers' three World Series appearances from 1907 to 1909, there were questions about whether the games were on the level.

After Detroit won its first American League pennant in 1907, there was a meeting with the three-man National Commission, two umpires and managers from the Tigers and the National League's pennant winners, the powerhouse Chicago Cubs. The players from both teams were represented at the meeting by Tiger second baseman Herman "Germany" Schaefer.

Schaefer was one of baseball's most legendary clowns. Stories of his goofy exploits on the diamond continue to be told more than a century after he retired, including his most famous stunt: stealing a base in reverse, going from second to first while the catcher held the ball, unsure where to throw it.

During the pre-Series meeting in Chicago's Auditorium Annex hotel, the participants discussed ground rules and how gate receipts would be divvied up. When it was suggested the players would get a cut of the receipts from the first four games, Schaefer piped in with an odd question: "Is a tie game considered a legal game?"

Schaefer insisted the players should share the gate receipts for the first five games, if one of the Series' initial four games ended in a tie. There had been no ties in the World Series up to that point, so the National Commission agreed with Schaefer's request.

In Game One, on October 8, the underdog Tigers took a 3–1 lead into the ninth inning. Then came sloppy—some say questionable—play.

Cub manager–first baseman Frank Chance led off the inning with a single. Tiger pitcher "Wild Bill" Donovan lived up to his name by plunking Chicago third baseman Harry Steinfeldt in the ribs, putting runners on first and second. Catcher Johnny Kling's successful bunt moved the tying runs into scoring position. Then, Tiger third baseman Bill Coughlin made an error on a ground ball by Cub second-sacker Johnny Evers, filling the bases.

Chicago right fielder Frank Schulte was out on a grounder to first base, although Chance scored on the play, closing the gap to 3–2. Donovan quickly got two strikes on pinch hitter George Howard before snapping off a curve, which umpire Hank O'Day called a strike.

The game would've been over, but the ball got past Tiger catcher Charlie "Boss" Schmidt, rolling several feet behind him. The passed ball allowed Steinfeldt to score the tying run. Evers then tried to steal home but was easily thrown out.

The two teams continued playing but did not score. Finally, after the twelfth inning, the game was called because of darkness.

The National Commission's decision to cut the players in on the extra game's gate receipts in the event of a tie had been reported, and some were suspicious of how the ninth inning played out.

"'More games, more dollars' was the polite thought the Cubs and Tigers bestowed upon a 3-to-3 score after twelve rounds of infuriated world's series baseball," was the lead in the next day's *San Francisco Chronicle* game story. "They share in the receipts until four complete games are played."

Attendance for Game One was 24,377, with total receipts of $29,162.50. The players' share was $15,747.75, or about $562.00 each—some $15,000.00 in 2019 terms. To modern multimillionaire ballplayers, fifteen grand wouldn't amount to much, but in 1907, the highest-paid player in baseball was Cleveland's Napoleon Lajoie, who made $8,500.00 a year, or about $228,000.00 in current money. Most players were far below that, in the $2,000.00 range. That extra $562.00 came in handy for Schmidt, Shaefer and the boys.

After the Series, with rumors percolating, the National Commission publicly brushed off Schaefer's question about a tie game as a mere coincidence—but baseball's governing board also moved quickly to establish a rule that in future World Series, the players would only share the gate receipts of the first four games, whether they ended in ties or not.

Did the Tigers and Cubs conspire to have Game One of the 1907 World Series end in a tie so they could pocket a few hundred extra dollars in gate receipts? A definitive answer will likely never be found, although at the time there were certainly those who bought into the theory.

IF THERE WERE WHISPERS about whether the 1907 World Series was on the level, reporters were screaming about it two years later, as the Tigers dropped their third straight Fall Classic, this time to the Pittsburgh Pirates.

Before, during and after the 1909 World Series (or "world's series," as it was referred to in those days), dozens of newspapers printed articles discussing the rumors of a fix. Most of the suspicion was aimed at Pittsburgh (which was then spelled "Pittsburg," without the "h"). The Pirates beat the Tigers in the first Series in history to go the full seven games. Some observers suggested that there was a nefarious reason the Series went the distance.

Canonsburg, Pennsylvania's the *Daily Notes* printed a bombshell article on October 13, 1909, following Game Four, discussing allegations that the players were throwing games to lengthen the World Series so they could pocket more gate receipts.

"That the world's championship series…is being manipulated from a box office standpoint, rather than on the principle that the best club shall win, is a charge which has been very actively circulated since Saturday's game at Forbes Field," the article read.

The story said that the rumors, which had persisted throughout the Series, really ramped up after Pirate player-manager Fred Clarke chose Howie Camnitz and Albert "Lefty" Leifield to pitch Games Two and Four, which the Tigers won. Both pitchers had posted outstanding regular-season records, with Leifield notching a 19-9 won-loss record with a 2.37 earned run average and Camnitz an even better at 25-6, 1.62. But they were horrible in the postseason: Camnitz's ERA was a whopping 13.50 during the Series, while Leifield's wasn't much better at 11.25.

One of the best-known sporting authorities in Pittsburg…placed the rumors in concrete form, saying: 'I am absolutely satisfied that the Pittsburg-Detroit games are being played for the box office instead of trying to honestly have determined which is the best club.…I have not met anyone who can explain why Camnitz was sent to the slab. That Camnitz was not physically fit for duty no one understood better than the officials of the Pittsburg baseball club. He had recently undergone an operation that resulted in greatly reducing his weight and vitality. Not only was he permitted to enter the box, but he was also kept there after his work disclosed the fact that he could not make good.

The article further quoted the unnamed gambler:

Pittsburg won Monday, so Leifield was put in today. He has been out of condition for weeks and could be depended on to maintain the box office equity. He did, though the game Mullin pitched would probably have won anyway. But with Leifield in the box for Pittsburg, nothing was left to chance. It now looks as though the next two games would break even, which will insure the playing off of the tie and conclude the entire series of seven games scheduled.

In response to the article, most other reporters shrugged off the suspicion, while the baseball establishment rushed to denounce the allegations.

"The presidents of the two leagues, the members of the national commission, and the managers of the two teams all brand as false stories that have been published asserting that the world's series is a frame-up," the *Indianapolis Star* reported. "The frame-up stories really sound very much like some of the hysterical ravings of an excited fan in the bleachers.

"The fact that Clarke pitched Camnitz and Leifield cannot be taken as evidence that he threw games to Detroit," the *Star* insisted. "August Hermann, president of the national commission, issued a statement demanding proof of the charges."

After the Series, a story in the *Washington Evening Star* picked up by newspapers across the country alleged that authorities in Detroit and Pittsburgh had looked the other way and allowed open betting.

"A glaring evil of the world's series was the gambling on the games," the *Evening Star* editorialized.

Betting reached proportions many times greater than ever before, and when the title is played for next year the chances are that the National Commission will ask for the aid of the police in cities represented by the contesting teams to drive the gamblers out of town. Thousands of dollars were bet openly in both Pittsburg and Detroit without the slightest effort on the part of the authorities to call a halt…encouraged by the failure of the police to even make a bluff to stop betting, the gamblers opened handbooks in the lobbies of the principle hotels at Detroit and made bets without the slightest interference.

The article singled out Pirate first baseman Bill Abstein for poor play and, in thinly veiled language, suggested he didn't play to win. "During the games with Detroit Abstein appeared to forget all that he knew about baseball. He ran the bases foolishly, made a number of costly errors, failed to hit well and disobeyed orders," the story said. "The other Pirates, seeing that Abstein was the 'goat'…kept up the cry against him, thus shifting some of the blame for their own bad playing. Before the series was ended, many of the Pirates shunned Abstein, and it was reported that he would be traded to some other team as speedily as possible."

Abstein, who had hit a paltry .231 in the Series, along with setting a record with nine strikeouts and committing several baserunning blunders, was placed on waivers shortly after the World Series ended.

The *St. Louis Post-Dispatch* published an article after the Series hinting that gamblers had influenced the outcome.

"What a change the betting underwent as the world's series progressed," the item said. "Beginning at almost 2 to 1, by the start of Saturday's final contest the speculation had switched to 10 to 8 on Detroit. The reason for this extreme change was not the prevailing belief that Detroit was the stronger, but the desire of the gamblers who were 'in bad' to hedge out."

As with the 1907 World Series, it's likely the question of whether the 1909 Fall Classic was on the up-and-up will never be definitively answered. And those two Series certainly weren't the only ones during that time to be stained by allegations of crookedness. But even for that less-strict era, when open gambling at ballparks was tolerated, there was a lot of talk about the 1909 Series being fixed.

TY COBB STARTED HIS baseball career in Detroit with a family controversy and ended it with a gambling scandal.

The game was only seven years removed from the devastating 1919 Black Sox scandal when, in November 1926, another gambling controversy surfaced that shocked the sporting world.

The scandal was exposed in increments. The first salvo, although it wasn't immediately recognized as such, came on November 4, 1926, when Detroiters awoke to the banner headline in the morning *Detroit Free Press*'s sports page: "Ty Cobb resigns as Tiger manager and George Moriarty succeeds him."

Cobb had been the Tigers' manager since 1921 and was a middling success, posting a .519 winning percentage and finishing as high as second place only once, so his resignation wasn't a total shock.

"To those who had their ears close to the ground, the change in the field leadership of the Tigers does not come as a surprise," the *Free Press* said.

Cobb told the Associated Press: "You know I am going to be 40 years old December 18. I am about as good as I ever was, but the time has come for me to quit taking chances, and that means that it is time for me to get out. I don't want to be one of those men who fade or have to be pushed out."

About three weeks later, on November 29, 1926, Cobb's longtime rival Tris Speaker announced he also was retiring from his post as player-manager for the Cleveland Indians. While rumors had swirled for some time that the man known as "The Gray Eagle" was planning to step down to pursue business ventures, Speaker's retirement was more of a surprise than Cobb's, since he'd guided the Indians to second place and had recorded a solid season, hitting .304 with fifty-two doubles.

"I am taking a vacation from baseball that I expect will last for the remainder of my life," Speaker told the Associated Press.

Then, on December 21, baseball commissioner Judge Kenesaw Mountain Landis dropped a nuclear bomb: He released to the newspapers more than one hundred pages of testimony outlining former Tiger pitcher Hubert "Dutch" Leonard's claim that in 1919 he had conspired with Cobb, Speaker and Cleveland outfielder Howard "Smoky Joe" Wood to fix a ball game. Landis said that letters between Cobb and Wood, in which they discussed placing a bet, indicated a possible fix.

The game in question, played on September 25, 1919, was won by the Tigers, 9–5. The Indians had clinched second place on September 24, and with no chance of catching the league-leading White Sox, they had nothing to play for. The Tigers, on the other hand, were fighting for third place—and a share of that year's World Series gate receipts. Prior to 1969, players on major-league teams that finished in the "first division," meaning first, second, third or fourth, received shares from the Fall Classic. The team that won the World Series netted 42 percent of the players' share; the team that lost the World Series got 28 percent; and the second-, third- and fourth-place teams in each league were awarded 7.5 percent, 5.0 percent and 2.5 percent, respectively.

If the three players had conspired to allow the Tigers to beat the Indians, it didn't show in the box score. Cobb was 1 for 5 with 1 RBI, while Speaker went 3 for 5 with 1 RBI. Wood, a once-great pitcher who hurt his arm and became a solid outfielder, didn't play.

Leonard had initially presented the two letters to Tiger owner Frank Navin and American League president Ban Johnson in May 1926, seven months before news of the allegations broke. Navin and Johnson tried to buy Leonard's silence, paying him $20,000 for the letters. On September 9, 1926, Johnson brought the matter to the American League's directors, who voted to turn over the evidence to Landis.

Johnson then confronted Cobb and Speaker about the matter and convinced them to retire. However, Landis, who'd been feuding with Johnson, launched his own investigation. He also made the decision to release the Wood allegations to the public—a move baseball historians believe was meant to humiliate Johnson.

Leonard's allegations were serious. He claimed that he, Speaker, Cobb and Wood had conspired to let the Tigers win the game before laying bets on Detroit. Leonard's only evidence was letters that had been sent to him by Cobb and Wood.

Cobb's letter, dated October 23, 1919, read:

Dear Dutch,

Well, old boy, guess you are out in California by this time and enjoying life.

I arrived home and found Mrs. Cobb only fair, but the baby girl was fine, and at this time Mrs. Cobb is very well, but I have been very busy getting acquainted with my family and have not tried to do any correspondence, hence my delay.

Wood and myself were considerably disappointed in our business proposition, as we had $2,000 to put into it, and the other side quoted us $1,400, and when we finally secured that much money it was about 2 o'clock and they refused to deal with us, as they had men in Chicago to take up the matter with and they had no time, so we completely fell down and of course we felt badly over it.

Everything was open to Wood and he can tell you about it when we get together. It was quite a responsibility and I don't care for it again, I can assure you.

Well, I hope you found everything in fine shape at home and all your troubles will be little ones. I have made this year's share of world series in cotton and expect to make more.

I thought the White Sox should have won but I am satisfied they were too overconfident. Well old scout, drop me a line when you can. We have had some dandy fishing since I arrived home.

With kindest regards to Mrs. Leonard, I remain,

Sincerely,

TY

Wood's undated letter to Leonard gave more details:

Dear Friend Dutch,

Enclosed please find certified check for sixteen hundred and thirty dollars ($1,630.00).

The only bet West could get down was $600 against $400 (10 to 7). Cobb did not get up a cent. He told us that and I believed him. Could have put up some at 5 to 2 on Detroit but did not as that would make us put up $1,000 to win $400.

We won the $420. I gave West $30, leaving $390 or $130 for each of us. Would not have cashed your check at all, but West thought he could get it up at 10 to 7, and I was going to put it all up at those odds. We would have won $1,750 for the $2,500 if we could have placed it.

If we ever have another chance like this we will know enough to try to get down early.

Let me hear from you, Dutch. With all good wishes to Mrs. Leonard and yourself, I am,
JOE WOOD

The story dominated headlines for weeks, with most papers taking the star players' side. They pointed out that Leonard had a grudge against Cobb for releasing him. Leonard also was sore at Speaker, an old friend, for not giving him a job after his release. Leonard was a talented pitcher—he still holds the record for the lowest ERA ever posted in a season, 0.96 in 1914, when he pitched for the Red Sox—but he also had a reputation as a clubhouse malcontent.

Support for Cobb and Speaker poured in from all circles, including the U.S. Congress. The accused players continually insisted they were innocent. Cobb released a written statement to the press:

Is there any decency left on earth? I'm beginning to doubt it. I know there is no gratitude. Here I am, after a lifetime in the game of hard, desperate and honest work forced to stand accused without ever having a chance to face my accuser. It is enough to try one's faith. I am branded a gambler on a ball game in which my club took part. I have never in the 22 years I have been in baseball made a single bet on an American League game.

The *Detroit Free Press* editorialized: "'Ty' Cobb has his faults and his shortcomings…but he is fundamentally honest, and though he may have been indiscreet and guilty of a small lapse in judgment back in 1919, nobody who is acquainted with him will ever believe he was a party to a crooked deal.…'Ty' simply isn't 'built that way.'"

Legendary humorist Will Rogers was among the celebrities who expressed support for Cobb and Speaker. "I want the world to know that I stand with Ty and Tris," Rogers said. "If they had been selling out all these years, I would have liked to have seen them play when they weren't selling."

Landis wanted Leonard to hop a train to Chicago to testify against Cobb, Wood and Speaker, but the ex-pitcher refused to leave his Fresno, California home. According to Landis, Leonard told him he didn't want to come to the Windy City, which at the time was controlled by mobster Al Capone, because, "they bump people off once in awhile there."

In the end, Landis cleared the three players. All he had was the word of a man who had motive to lie and letters that made it appear that some bets indeed had taken place but didn't really prove anything.

"These players have not been found, nor are they now guilty of 'framing' a ball game," Landis said in a statement released on January 27, 1927. "By no decent system of justice could such a finding be made. Therefore, they are not placed on the ineligible list."

Cobb's career was done in Detroit, however. The following season, he signed with the Philadelphia Athletics, playing two more years before hanging up his spikes following the 1928 season. Speaker signed with the Washington Senators for one year and then joined Cobb on the A's for his final season, 1928.

Johnson had seen his influence wane since baseball's owners appointed Landis as the sport's first commissioner and gave him absolute power in an attempt to restore public trust in the wake of the crooked 1919 World Series. The Cobb-Speaker affair was the final humiliation for Johnson, who resigned following the 1927 season.

Did Leonard's accusations have merit? There certainly is evidence that Cobb, Speaker and Wood bet on baseball, but nothing supports the charge that they fixed the game. Pete Rose was banned from the game for essentially the same infraction: betting on baseball with no proof he ever gave less than his best on the field. But because of Landis's power struggle with Johnson—and the fact that the commissioner likely didn't want another scandal to sully the sport so soon after the Black Sox affair—Cobb and Speaker were welcomed back into the game. Cobb was a member of the first Baseball Hall of Fame class in 1936, and Speaker was enshrined the following year.

The subject of the scandal remained a sore spot with Cobb. After Cobb's death in 1961, J.G. Taylor Spink, legendary publisher of the *Sporting News* and a longtime Cobb friend, said he wrote a letter to the Georgia Peach in 1958 inquiring about the controversy. According to Spink, Cobb wrote back:

> *Taylor, even to the most wonderful friend I have in the world, which you are, my lips are still sealed on this matter. This is an honor thing with me. It is just too distasteful to talk about. I think it is too late now to stir up things. Most of the people involved are now dead. It almost killed me to suffer such dishonor in a game which I loved so much and to which I think I gave so much. I admit the whole thing rankles me and I talk too much. Someday I'll tell the story which has some twists which would intrigue even your reportorial heart, but not now.*

For the next five decades, baseball was free of any major gambling controversies. Then, the February 23, 1970 issue of *Sports Illustrated* hit the newsstands, scandalizing another Detroit Tiger superstar.

The article was titled: "Denny McLain and the Mob."

4

DENNY'S DOWNFALL

Rules? Laws? They were for the other guys. Not for Denny McLain. In his first game as a professional with the Class D Harlan (Kentucky) Smokies, McLain threw a no-hitter. He lost his second game, although he allowed no earned runs and struck out sixteen batters. Then, he reportedly broke the team's rules by leaving to visit his girlfriend on an off day. If that wasn't enough, he infuriated his hometown fans by calling Harlan a "hick town."

Great pitching, rule-breaking and controversy would come to define McLain's brief, brilliant career before it all came crashing down around him in one of the swiftest, most spectacular falls from grace in sports history.

Dennis Dale McLain was born on March 29, 1944, in Markham, Illinois, a small town about twenty-five miles south of Chicago. He said he grew up fearing the wrath of his abusive father, Tom.

The pitching talent was there from the start, as McLain dominated Little League and Babe Ruth League. He got a baseball scholarship to attend Mount Carmel High School in Chicago, which he led to three city championships. The fireballing right-hander racked up a high school pitching record of 38-7, and when he graduated in June 1962, he signed with the Chicago White Sox for a $10,000 bonus, with another $7,000 promised if he made the major leagues.

After his two spectacular debut games for the Harlan Smokies, McLain was promoted to the Clinton (Iowa) C-Sox in the Class D Midwest League. He had several unauthorized absences from the team, costing himself hundreds of dollars in fines.

At the beginning of the 1963 season, the White Sox left McLain unprotected, as players with a year of minor-league service were susceptible to the draft if they weren't promoted to the majors. Rather than promote McLain, the White Sox chose to protect fellow pitchers Bruce Howard and Dave DeBusschere, a Detroit native who would later pitch for the White Sox before going on to star with the Detroit Pistons and New York Knicks in the National Basketball Association.

The Tigers scooped up the unprotected McLain, and he began the 1963 season with the Duluth-Superior Dukes, where he used his overpowering fastball and slider to notch a 13-2 record with a 2.55 ERA and 157 strikeouts in just 141 innings. McLain was promoted to the Knoxville Smokies in the Double-A South Atlantic (Sally) League, posting a 5-4 record in 11 starts.

McLain was called up to the parent club, and in his September 21 major-league debut in Tiger Stadium, he faced his former team, the White Sox. McLain threw a complete game, scattering 7 hits, for a 4–3 win. The first run of the game came in the fifth inning, when the rookie pitcher slammed an opposite-field home run off Chicago pitcher Fritz Ackley—the only home run of McLain's major-league career. McLain also picked off two baserunners in his debut.

By 1965, McLain was finding his groove, posting a 16-6 record with a 2.61 earned run average and 192 strikeouts, good for third in the American League behind Cleveland pitcher Sam McDowell and teammate Mickey Lolich.

McLain became a star in 1966. With a 13-4 midseason record, he was chosen to start the All-Star Game in St. Louis. He worked three innings, retiring all nine batters he faced on just twenty-eight pitches. McLain finished the season 20-14 with a 3.92 ERA.

His ascent continued in 1967, although the way he ended the season would later be the subject of a national controversy.

McLain had seventeen wins by September 18, when he told team officials that he had injured two toes on his left foot. "McLain, knocked out in his last four starts, said he dozed off while watching television at his home Monday and injured his foot when he arose from a chair," the Associated Press reported.

"The foot fell asleep on me and when I got up it just collapsed outwards," McLain told the AP. "I don't know if anyone will believe it, but that's what happened."

Some expressed doubt about McLain's story, prompting him to defend himself to *Detroit Free Press* columnist Joe Falls. When Falls told him some people didn't believe his excuse, McLain said. "I know it. But what am I going to do—make up a story? Tell them I smashed my foot kicking something? It happened just like I said it did.…[H[ow could I make up a story like that? It's too crazy. It really happened. I know the manager is sore at me but what can I do? I got hurt and couldn't help it."

Meanwhile, the Tigers had a pennant race to worry about. They were in the thick of the closest battle in baseball history, with Detroit, Boston, Chicago and Minnesota all within a few games of one another as the season careened into its final days.

Tiger manager Mayo Smith took a swipe at McLain when he told reporters he had picked his pitching rotation for the last series of the season against the California Angels. "It'll be (Joe) Sparma, (Earl) Wilson and (Mickey) Lolich—providing none of them falls off a sofa," the skipper told the *Free Press*.

Despite Smith's quip, he later named McLain to pitch the season finale, the second game of a doubleheader at Tiger Stadium. If the Tigers could win, they'd force a one-game playoff with the Red Sox to determine who would go to the World Series.

McLain was ineffective, pitching two and two-thirds innings and giving up three earned runs before he was yanked in the third inning. The Tigers would go on to lose to the Angels, 8–5.

McLain's injury proved fatal for the Tigers' pennant chances, as he didn't win a game after August 29. Had he won just one of his final four starts, the Tigers would have at least tied the Red Sox. Instead, after Tiger second baseman Dick McAuliffe grounded into a double play to end the season—the only double play McAuliffe hit into all year—Detroit and McLain were left to mutter "wait 'til next year."

Angry Tiger fans swarmed the field, wreaking havoc and ripping out home plate, the pitcher's rubber and huge patches of grass.

THE 1968 SEASON WAS dubbed "The Year of the Pitcher," and while other pitchers, most notably the Cardinals' Bob Gibson, posted superior peripheral statistics, no pitcher was more celebrated that season than the thirty-game winner, McLain.

The cocky, twenty-four-year-old Illinois native started the season 5-0 and had a 16-2 record by the All-Star break. He finished at 31-6, making him only one of 21 pitchers since 1901 to eclipse the 30-win mark. With five-man pitching rotations, it's unlikely there'll be another 30-game winner in the big leagues.

McLain had been a successful pitcher prior to 1968, but that year, his stardom shot into the stratosphere. He regularly appeared on national television, grinning, joking and playing the Hammond organ. He was a licensed pilot and began flying to road games in his own chartered planes, irking teammates.

"The rules for Denny just don't seem to be the same as for the rest of us," catcher Bill Freehan would write the following season in his memoir, *Behind the Mask*.

But winning covers up a multitude of sins, and Tiger management allowed McLain to "do his thing." He faltered early during the World Series against the St. Louis Cardinals, losing his first two starts before finally winning Game Six.

After the Tigers beat the Cards in seven games, coming back from a 3-1 Series deficit, the accolades for McLain continued rolling in, as he won both the Cy Young and Most Valuable Player Awards.

Although he didn't match his historic 1968 season, McLain had another fine year in 1969, going 24-9 with a 2.80 ERA to win his second consecutive Cy Young Award, although this time he shared the honor with Baltimore Orioles pitcher Mike Cuellar.

As the new decade dawned, McLain was at the pinnacle. Only twenty-five, he was one of the top pitchers in baseball. With his off-field activities, including national talk-show gigs and playing the organ in Las Vegas, he earned more money than anyone in the game.

Then, with the 1970s only a month old, the crash came—as swift as it was spectacular, like something out of an Aesop's fable.

THE STORM CLOUDS BEGAN gathering on Valentine's Day 1970, when the *Detroit Free Press* published a front-page article quoting baseball commissioner Bowie Kuhn, who said his office was reviewing "certain off-field activities of Denny McLain that occurred in 1967."

The *Free Press* story also said McLain was cooperating with Detroit FBI officials in a gambling investigation.

The next day, the *Detroit News* revealed that McLain was actually a target of the federal probe, that the pitcher had alleged ties to Flint bookmakers and that the fishy-sounding toe injury during the 1967 pennant race was under renewed scrutiny.

"There is no question that the brilliant pitching career of the 26-year-old McLain is hanging in the balance," the article stated. The story revealed that Detroit FBI agents had questioned McLain "for several hours" earlier that week.

"Last week, after 2½ years, there was a revival of interest in McLain's [1967] toe injury," the article said. "Dr. Clarence Livingood, one of the Tigers' two team physicians, phoned the office of Dr. Russell Wright, the other Tiger doctor, and asked for the hospital report on the injury."

The *News* quoted a "highly placed law enforcement official," who said: "McLain's injury didn't happen in his home. It hurts when you get stomped for not doing something you are supposed to do. A fellow won a big bet and didn't get paid off."

According to the article, "several sports writers clearly recall McLain, in 1967, phoning basketball and horse bets from the Tigers dressing room in Lakeland, Fla. to a man in Flint."

The story also discussed the star pitcher's mounting money woes. "McLain's financial problems on a salary of $90,000 plus lucrative night club engagements have long been public knowledge," the *News* reported. "He is being sued by a number of creditors and a $8,400 lien has been placed on his home by the Internal Revenue Service. Oakland County Circuit Court records indicate his total debt is about $50,000.

"But it was not made public until Saturday that the pitcher's financial affairs are so tangled that he will be drawing no pay checks from the Tigers until late this coming season," the *News* continued. "His salary checks are being mailed directly to the Detroit Bank & Trust Co. under a plan to consolidate his debts, according to Alex Callam, Tigers business manager."

The article also revealed that *Sports Illustrated* was working on its own investigative story about McLain's alleged mob involvement.

THE FEBRUARY 23, 1970 edition of *Sports Illustrated* set the baseball world on its ear. The cover photo was a headshot of McLain staring off to the left, accompanied by the headline: "Denny McLain and the Mob, Baseball's Big Scandal."

According to the story (which actually hit the newsstands on February 18, five days before the cover date), McLain in 1967 had invested in a gambling operation based in a Flint, Michigan restaurant, the Short Horn Steakhouse. McLain's partner in the bookmaking venture was "Jiggs" Gazell, who was tied in with "a Syrian mob with Cosa Nostra connections," the magazine reported.

The article said that McLain and Gazell were put under "heavy pressure" in August and September 1967, when a gambler named Edward Voshen netted $46,000 from a race won by a four-year-old colt named Williamston Kid. Voshen's bookie couldn't pay off the winnings and told the gambler to find the bookie's partners, McLain and Gazell.

After several months of trying to get paid, Voshen, who ran a Battle Creek, Michigan truck stop, enlisted the aid of infamous Detroit mobster Anthony Giacalone, who, according to *Sports Illustrated*'s sources, met with McLain in early September. The magazine claimed that Giacalone stomped McLain's foot, dislocating his toes. The mobster threatened more pain if the pitcher didn't pay up.

Voshen never did get his money. He was killed on October 16, 1968, in a car crash outside Battle Creek.

The day the *Sports Illustrated* article was published, the *Detroit News* quoted Flint police chief James W. Rutherford, who said his department had investigated McLain in 1967 and had gotten reports that the pitcher had his foot "stomped on" by Giacalone aboard his boat.

"McLain was supposed to pay the money to the Giacalones," Rutherford told the *News*. "He didn't pay, however, so they took him on the boat in Lake St. Clair. They were going to break both McLain's hands, but they decided they would never get their money if they broke McLain's hands. Instead, the Giacalones stomped on his toe."

Sports Illustrated, quoting a mob source, said: "Just prior to McLain's toe injury, Billy Giacalone had made big bets on the Red Sox and the Twins to win the pennant and later bet heavily against the Tigers in McLain's final start."

Hours after the *Sports Illustrated* story was published, reporters found McLain on a Lakeland, Florida golf course. He called the allegations made in the article "absurd" and said he planned on bringing a lawsuit.

"I'm not talking about just one suit, but many," McLain told the *News*.

Reporters hounded the other Tigers, who didn't hide their disdain. "I think Denny owes his teammates an explanation," Freehan told the *News*. "It's unfair for us to have to answer questions when we haven't heard his side of the story. There are two schools of thought on this ball club. I'd say the feeling is split about 50-50 on whether Denny's right or wrong."

Just before spring training in 1970, Commissioner Bowie Kuhn suspended McLain indefinitely. Following the announcement, McLain apologized while still denying the allegations.

"All I can say is I'm very sorry, I caused a lot of people a lot of embarrassment," he told the Associated Press. "My immediate problem is getting a job. I'm in financial trouble. What am I going to do for money? I've got a family to take care of."

McLain also predicted that he'd be reinstated within a month. But on April 1, Kuhn announced that the suspension would last until July 1, nearly half the season.

During a press conference, Kuhn read aloud a statement exonerating McLain from the worst allegations, claiming the pitcher had just been a gullible pawn of gamblers.

"While McLain believed he had become a partner in this [bookmaking] operation and has so admitted to me…it would appear that he was the victim of a confidence scheme," the commissioner said. "I would thus conclude that McLain was never a partner and had no proprietary interest in the bookmaking operation. The fair inference is that his own gullibility and avarice had permitted him to become a dupe of the gamblers with whom he associated."

Kuhn also said that McLain's actions didn't affect the 1967 pennant race. "There is no evidence to indicate that McLain gave less than his best effort at any time while performing for the Detroit Tigers," the commissioner said. "There is no evidence that McLain in 1967 or subsequently has been guilty of any misconduct involving baseball or the playing of baseball games."

After the commissioner read his statement, a reporter asked him the difference between McLain trying to become a bookmaker and becoming one. "I think you have to consider the difference is the same as between murder and attempted murder," Kuhn replied.

The local and national press lambasted what they considered a light punishment by Kuhn.

"It will be easier for some to believe that McLain was far more deeply involved and that Kuhn, acting for what he conceived to be the good of the game, ended his inquiry before it would lead to prosecution in open court and public disillusion," wrote Robert Lipsyte of the *New York Times*.

"Sure of its knowledge of self-purity, baseball has now put its head back in the sand," wrote *Miami Herald* columnist Edwin Pope. "Commissioner Kuhn has lightly flicked McLain on the wrist and given him a benediction as an honest but misguided dumbbell. I think his decision is outrageously mild. It is a disgraceful compromise."

The *Flint Journal*'s editorial page raged:

> *Baseball has suffered a severe setback.…McLain's association with gamblers and his decision to try to profit from that association throws a dark shadow over every pitch McLain has thrown.… [T]hat shadow does not stop at the mound at Tiger Stadium, it is spread across all professional*

baseball. At a time when cynicism among young [people] *is already too widespread, McLain and Kuhn have provided new cause for such cynicism and have, between them, dealt baseball a vicious blow.*

In his 2007 autobiography *I Told You I Wasn't Perfect*, McLain said he was distracted during the 1967 season. "I was spooked about the ghost of Ed Voshen and worried about being exposed," he wrote. "I kept expecting someone to tap me on the shoulder and say, 'Hey, where's my money?' or that my car was going to blow up."

THE TUMBLE FROM MOUNT Olympus continued as the 1970 season played out, with McLain picking up two more suspensions. Meanwhile, creditors were closing in; the furniture in his home was seized by the IRS to satisfy a $9,460 tax bill.

As expected, the two-time defending Cy Young Award winner returned from his gambling-related suspension on July 1 to a packed Tiger Stadium. The party was ruined when the Yankees scored five runs against McLain, who didn't make it out of the sixth inning.

Then, on August 28, McLain was suspended by the Tigers for seven games after dousing two Tiger beat writers—the *Detroit Free Press*'s Jim Hawkins and the *Detroit News*' Watson Spoelstra—with ice water before a home game against the Oakland A's.

McLain got Hawkins first, pouring the water on him while the writer sat in the Tiger clubhouse. According to Hawkins, McLain said, "I'm going to get all you guys…and I'd like to throw all of you one by one into the whirlpool before this season is over, too."

About forty minutes later, a Tiger Stadium security guard went to the press box and told Spoelstra that McLain wanted to see him in the clubhouse. When the reporter went to see what was up, McLain complained about a headline and poured a bucket of water over his head, too.

Tiger GM Jim Campbell suspended McLain "for an indefinite period not to exceed 30 days for conduct unbecoming a professional baseball player."

Less than a week later, Kuhn found out that McLain had brought a gun onto a team flight in August, and the commissioner suspended the pitcher for the rest of the season.

Three strikes, and Denny was out. The Tigers traded him to the Washington Senators a few days after the 1970 season was over in what would prove to be a heist for Detroit. The players the Tigers got included third baseman Aurelio Rodriguez, shortstop Eddie Brinkman and pitcher Joe Coleman, who would win twenty games twice for Detroit.

After the press conference announcing the trade, Tiger GM Jim Campbell threw a package of TUMS anti-acid pills into the wastebasket and told reporters, "I won't be needing these anymore."

The Senators acquired a pitcher who would prove washed up just a year after being at baseball's pinnacle. On top of that, McLain's attitude was worse than his 10-22 record. He was constantly agitating manager Ted Williams, one of the greatest hitters of all time and himself no shrinking violet. McLain was the leader of a group of clubhouse malcontents called the "Underminer's Club."

Washington dumped McLain following the 1971 season. The Atlanta Braves and Oakland A's would later hope for a McLain comeback. But he was through, an out-of-shape has-been when he retired from baseball at age twenty-nine.

During his first few years out of the game, McLain was involved in various moneymaking ventures that didn't pan out, including investing in Projector Beam Sales Inc., a Tampa big-screen television firm; working for a mortgage broker; running a bar; and opening two walk-in medical clinics in Florida. McLain also hustled money at golf courses.

In 1975, McLain was hired as general manager for the minor-league Memphis Blues. Less than a year later, he was fired after he ran up the team's debt from $200,000 to $340,000, including $53,000 he owed the IRS for unpaid Social Security and withholding taxes.

When his business ventures lost money, leaving behind a trail of creditors, lawsuits and tax liens, McLain turned to the underworld. He started loansharking and bookmaking. He reportedly once was given a suitcase filled with $160,000 in cash to fly a man convicted of manslaughter out of the country in his airplane.

Eventually, it all caught up with him.

In March 1984, the U.S. Department of Justice indicted McLain and six of his associates on charges of conspiracy to smuggle more than four hundred kilos of cocaine and racketeering involving loansharking and extortion, along with other crimes.

According to the indictment, McLain accepted a $7,000 check on September 8, 1982, from a drug dealer to install an extra fuel tank on his plane to facilitate the smuggling of cocaine. Six weeks later, federal agents shot the plane up after the pilot reportedly tried to run down an officer on the airstrip. The plane was seized by federal authorities.

McLain's co-defendants Barry Nelson and Larry Knott would later plead guilty; Nelson pleaded to racketeering, while Knott pleaded guilty to possession of cocaine with intent to distribute. Knott claimed he and McLain delivered cocaine in golf bags in Fort Lauderdale in 1982.

The indictment also accused McLain of using a mortgage-lending firm, Tampa Mortgage and Loan, as a front for a loansharking, racketeering and gambling operation. The FBI said he and his partners would loan money at 150 percent interest and that McLain threatened people for not paying. McLain also was charged with taking kickbacks on loans and facilitating illegal bets on football and basketball.

At McLain's trial, his attorney, Arnold Levine, portrayed his client as Commissioner Kuhn had—a gullible athlete who was snookered by more experienced criminals.

"You're going to find that Denny McLain was a victim, not a participant," Levine said during his opening statement in a Tampa federal courtroom. "It's obviously easy to take a fall once you're used to the public acclaim and the public attention."

McLain took the witness stand and confessed to running a bookmaking operation out of Tampa Mortgage and Loan. He denied being a drug smuggler but admitted that his leased plane had been used to transport cocaine between Florida and New Jersey.

While on the stand, McLain claimed the shock of being indicted led him to contemplate killing himself. When his attorney asked why he didn't go through with the suicide, McLain said: "In all candor, two reasons: I'm innocent of the charges, and the day I thought of [committing suicide], I couldn't find the bullets."

On March 16, 1985, following a fourteen-week trial, a jury deliberated for three days before convicting McLain on racketeering, extortion and cocaine possession. He was found not guilty on the charge of conspiracy to smuggle cocaine.

The following month, U.S. district judge Elizabeth A. Kovachevich sentenced McLain to twenty-three years in prison. Prior to sentencing, the former pitcher told the court: "I don't know how you get to where I was today from where I was 17 years ago [in 1968]." He then answered his own question, saying he was in his situation because of "greed, avarice, a lot of bad judgment and trying to make a fast dollar.

"I'll pay for my conviction the rest of my life," McLain told the judge. "I've gone through a lot of shame and disgrace, and no sentence can equal the humiliation of being handcuffed in front of television cameras."

McLain was sent to the Talladega Correctional Facility in Alabama but, within a few months, was sent to the Atlanta Federal Penitentiary, where he told the prison baseball team, the Cardinals, that he was available to pitch. The offer was refused, so other inmates formed their own team, the Detroit Dennys, and asked McLain to pitch and manage the club. In his first and only game, he gave up four runs in five and two-thirds innings and told the *Detroit Free Press* the outing had taken a toll.

"I feel like I had been at Pearl Harbor and survived," he said. "I can guarantee you as of this date, this hour, this minute, I am retired."

In August 1987, McLain got a break when the Atlanta-based Eleventh U.S. Circuit Court of Appeals ruled that McLain was entitled to a new trial. The appellate judges ruled that trial judge Kovachevich had unfairly rushed McLain's trial. The appeals court also criticized the trial prosecutor for insulting a defense lawyer in front of the jury.

In order to avoid a second trial, McLain pleaded guilty to racketeering and cocaine possession charges. Kovachevich sentenced him to twelve years but ordered him released on five years' probation because of the time he'd already served.

In December 1988, McLain walked out of the courthouse a free man.

"We're elated—it's an early Christmas present," McLain, accompanied by his wife, Sharyn, and four children, told the Associated Press. "I had no idea what to expect. I'm just going to try to get on with the rest of my life."

McLain vowed to make the most of his second chance. It wouldn't be the last time he'd break a promise.

WHEN HE GOT OUT of prison, McLain cashed in on his name by taking a job as promotion director for the Fort Wayne Komets of the International Hockey League, although it didn't last long, because he constantly fought with management. McLain also published a book he'd written while in prison, *Strikeout*, the first of three autobiographies he would release.

In 1989, McLain got yet another break. He began hosting a morning talk show on 1270 AM in Detroit, and it became a surprising success, which he parlayed into a TV gig, teaming with sportscaster Eli Zaret for the *Eli and Denny* show.

McLain invested in Peet Packing, a meatpacking company near Flint, Michigan, in 1993. Three years later, McLain and his business partner, Robert Smigiel, were indicted by a federal grand jury on charges that they stole more than $3 million from Peet's pension fund, using the money for personal investments and to pay off company debts.

McLain and Smigiel got themselves appointed as trustees of Peet's $12 million employee pension fund, skirting company rules requiring trustees to be banks. They, along with co-conspirator Jeffrey Egan, a financial advisor, transferred $3.06 million from the fund into the accounts of two shell companies. The scheme was exposed when bank officers and union officials began questioning the pension accounts.

In May 1997, McLain was sentenced to eight years in prison. This time, he declined to make a statement to the court.

McLain's long-suffering wife, Sharyn, divorced him the day he started his prison sentence.

A *Port Huron Times Herald* op-ed that ran the day after McLain was sentenced was scathing:

> *Denny McLain was a hero to a generation of Detroit Tiger fans for his pitching, particularly in the championship year of 1968. Today, he's heading to prison—for the second time. Drugs or booze weren't his downfall. His nemesis was greed. He and a partner took over the Peet Packing Co., sucked it dry, left its pensioners with nothing and tried to walk away. See you, Denny. You were something in 1968. You're still something: a disgraced crook.*

MCLAIN WOULD SERVE SIX years in prison before being released in 2003. He would bounce from job to job, mostly sales gigs. He remarried Sharyn after he said he got down on his knees and begged her forgiveness.

In 2007, McLain and his former TV co-host Zaret published the pitcher's third autobiography *I Told You I Wasn't Perfect*, in which he threw teammates under the bus. He said Tiger legend Al Kaline "wasn't the most loved SOB in the clubhouse" and that the other Tigers resented Kaline for turning down a $100,000 salary offer from management because it cost the other players money.

There would be more lawsuits and arrests. In 2011, McLain was charged with bilking a Louisiana landowner out of money he owed for scrap metal. McLain was arrested when he mistakenly drove onto the Canadian side of the Blue Water Bridge near Port Huron, Michigan. When an officer ran his name, he saw there was a warrant for his arrest in Louisiana. McLain was taken into custody, but the charges were dropped within a few days.

McLain was hired for a few Detroit-area radio gigs, but none of them came close to matching his earlier on-air success. He supported himself by writing a column for a Detroit sports magazine and appearing at card shows.

On September 8, 2018, the Tigers staged a celebration at Comerica Park to commemorate the fiftieth anniversary of the 1968 world championship. The World Series heroes, now paunchy and gray, were introduced one-by-one as they lumbered out of the dugout to the stage.

McLain received a rousing applause when his name was called. He used a cane to limp across the blue walkway toward the stage that was set up at second base, tipping his cap to the crowd while Cream's "Sunshine of Your Love," blasted from the ballpark speakers.

As part of the anniversary celebration, the Tigers in 2018 gave away a series of bobbleheads featuring 1968 heroes Al Kaline, Bill Freehan, Willie Horton and Mickey Lolich.

McLain, perhaps the most glaring symbol of the Tigers' success that year, was not honored with a bobblehead.

5

FELONIOUS FELINES

olice and court records are peppered with the names of former Detroit Tigers who committed crimes ranging from the humorous to the heinous.

RED SAID DEMON RUM made him do it.

Jerry "Red" Downs is a nondescript figure in Tiger history. The redheaded second baseman was a backup player for the pennant-winning 1907–8 teams before bouncing around the majors for a few years. Downs then managed minor league clubs, including the San Francisco Seals in the Pacific Coast League, but he would later say his alcoholism drove him from the game.

By the time the Great Depression hit, Downs was at rock bottom. In 1932, the New York Giants held spring training in Los Angeles, and he visited friends on the team who were staying at the luxurious Biltmore Hotel. When Downs walked inside, he spotted the Everard Jewelry Store in the lobby and hatched a plan to rob it.

On March 19, 1932, Downs and accomplice Edward Carlson pulled off a brazen caper. "The robbery, sensational in its daring, was staged while scores of pedestrians walked by the entrance of the jewelry shop, which opens into the lobby of the fashionable hotel," United Press reported.

The robbers walked into the store brandishing pistols. The two men tied up the store manager and the clerk with cord that resembled fishing tackle. "Rubber balls were placed in their mouths for gags," the UP reported.

Downs and Carlson cleaned out the shelves and the safe, which happened to be open, and walked out of the hotel and into LA's busy theater district with $52,000 in jewelry and cash (nearly $900,000 in current money).

Los Angeles detectives checked with their underworld sources and heard street talk that a man named Eugene Jones had been flashing a lot of jewelry. Police tracked him down in a hotel, found the stolen merchandise and arrested him. Jones cut a deal and fingered the men who sold him the jewels: Downs and Carlson. The robbers were arrested and confessed to the crime.

"Liquor has put me out for the third time," Downs told an LA detective, according to the *Los Angeles Times*. "First it caused me to lose a place in the big league, where I might, by this time, have been a successful manager. The second time it threw me out of the Coast League. And now it's got me into this jam."

Downs was convicted of first-degree robbery and sentenced to between five years and life. He served his prison sentence in San Quentin for more than three years before being paroled in December 1935. "A Christmas parole was assured today to Jerry Downs," the *Los Angeles Times* said.

Less than four years later, liquor would apparently put the fifty-six-year-old Downs out for the fourth and final time. On October 19, 1939, the former ballplayer died in Council Bluffs, Iowa, of cirrhosis of the liver.

DURING HIS ELEVEN YEARS in the big leagues, Jerry Priddy was a great defensive second baseman with some pop in his bat and cock in his walk. After his career, he tried his hand at acting. When Hollywood didn't come calling, Priddy cooked up a real-life caper worthy of a movie script: a comedy about a bumbling criminal.

While Priddy isn't exactly a household name, noted baseball historian Bill James discusses him at length in his book *The Politics of Glory*. James called Priddy one of the greatest defensive players in history, ranking him as the seventy-third best second baseman of all time.

When the tall, blond Priddy and future Hall of Fame shortstop Phil Rizzuto came up through the Yankee minor-league system in the early 1940s as the highly touted keystone combination of the future, Priddy was considered the better prospect. Legendary Yankee broadcaster Mel Allen regularly gave updates about the pair as they worked their way through the farm system.

Priddy had an ego to match the hype. Rizzuto recalled that the first day Priddy walked into the Yankee training camp, he told Joe Gordon, New York's established second baseman, that he was better at the position.

Gordon ended up in the Hall of Fame. Priddy ended up in prison.

Priddy was a solid major-league ballplayer, but his heart was in Hollywood. Throughout his baseball career, he kept contact with the movie industry. In 1942, he served on the Paramount studio technical crew for the Bing Crosby movie *Dixie*.

While he was with the Tigers, Priddy served as a technical advisor for the 1952 movie *The Winning Team*, a biography of Hall of Fame pitcher Grover Cleveland Alexander. Future president Ronald Reagan played the troubled pitcher, and Doris Day was his romantic interest. In one scene, Priddy reportedly put a pillow under his shirt and appeared as an extra as Babe Ruth.

Priddy appeared in three other movies: *The Stratton Story* (1949), *Kill the Umpire* (1950) and *Three Little Words* (1950), according to the Internet Movie Database. He also appeared on *The Colgate Comedy Hour*, a variety show that aired on NBC from 1950 to 1955.

Priddy was with Detroit from 1950 to 1953. He hit .267 as a Tiger, solid for a middle infielder, with a .355 on-base percentage (OBP). He also showed great glove work at second base. His best seasons arguably were with the Tigers, but his career was effectively ended by a gruesome ankle injury at home plate in July 1952. He was done for the season and played only a handful of games the following year before the Tigers released him.

His big-league days were done, but Priddy bounced around the minors for a few years as a player and a manager before retiring in 1956. He made overtures to Hollywood, hoping for an executive position, but nobody gave him a job.

In 1959, Priddy, a solid amateur golfer, joined the PGA tour, after Bob McCulloch, owner of the McCulloch Motors car dealership in Los Angeles, sponsored him. Priddy failed there, too, earning only $1,105.54 in the first year of a golf career that ended the next season.

Priddy moved from sports into other ventures that flopped. He opened a restaurant with California disc jockey Ray York. When that fizzled out, the ex-ballplayer went into the paper business, becoming vice-president of the DeHater Paper Corporation in 1963 before opening his own company, Priddy Paper Products, which supplied the restaurant industry. Priddy named fellow Los Angeles native and major-league outfielder George "Catfish" Metkovich as his vice-president.

In 1971, Priddy opened an advertising firm, Jerry Priddy and Associates, in Burbank. However, within a few years, that, too, was failing.

Running out of options, Priddy conjured up a get-rich-quick scheme that could generously be described as poorly planned.

On June 5, 1973, he placed seven phone calls to the Princess Cruises Los Angeles office, claiming there were four timed explosives aboard the *Island Princess*, which had shipped out of Long Beach with 525 passengers and 325 crew members aboard. The ship was about two hundred miles south of San Diego on a seven-day pleasure cruise to Puerto Vallarta, Mexico, when Priddy warned that if Princess Cruises didn't pay him $250,000 in cash, he would detonate the bombs.

Priddy told cruise-line officials to drop off the cash in a garbage can in an alley behind his Burbank advertising office at 4404 Riverside Drive.

Crew members searched the ship and found two packages about the size of cigarette packs wrapped in brown paper. The packages, which were on the ship's bridge and in the engine room, were thrown overboard, and it was never determined if they were incendiary.

"We'll never know what [the packages] contained," a spokesman for the cruise line told the Associated Press. "The ship has been completely searched. We feel the ship is secure."

Hours after placing the calls, Priddy ventured into the alley behind his office to pick up his booty—which, unbeknownst to him, was a paper bag filled with bill-sized pieces of paper.

FBI agents were lying in wait. They testified that they watched Priddy "approaching the trash can several times and glancing about for two hours before suddenly darting out and seizing a brown paper bundle," United Press International reported.

Priddy was arrested and charged in federal court with extortion, a felony that carried up to twenty years in prison and a $10,000 fine. He pleaded not guilty and was released on $150,000 bond.

During his trial, Priddy admitted he'd phoned in the bomb threat—but he claimed he was forced to do it. He testified that a man with a "Mexican accent" threatened to kill him and his family if he didn't phone in the threat to the cruise line.

Prosecutors said Priddy fabricated the story, insisting he initiated the extortion scheme because his advertising business was failing.

The jury wasn't buying Priddy's story, either, and after nearly five hours of deliberations, the panel of ten women and two men came back with a guilty verdict.

Prior to issuing his sentence on January 16, 1974, U.S. district judge Irving Hill ripped into the former ballplayer. "We are dealing with a crime of very great seriousness," the judge said. "When somebody threatens the lives of innocent men and women and children…that stirs very deep emotions and requires strong treatment."

Priddy then addressed the court. "For the mistakes I've made, I feel I've suffered," he said. "I would ask to be allowed to go back into the society to which I owe so much."

Despite the judge's acerbic language, he handed down a fairly light sentence of nine months in prison.

After the hearing, Priddy declined further comment to reporters other than to ask, "Who am I to criticize the court?"

Priddy served only about half his sentence in Terminal Island Federal Correction Institute before being paroled. After his release, it was reported that he was penniless, since his bank had seized his assets to satisfy a debt.

It's unclear how Priddy made ends meet during the final years of his life.

On the morning of March 3, 1980, Priddy ate breakfast in his North Hollywood home. When he stood up from the table, he suffered a massive heart attack and died. He was sixty.

CHAD CURTIS WAS THE local boy who made good. The pride of Middleville, Michigan, scraped his way to the big leagues, despite his five-foot, ten-inch, 175-pound frame, and enjoyed a long, productive career.

It was a feel-good story with a disgraceful ending.

Curtis, whose most prominent features were his Biff Tannen–like crewcut and his ever-present "What Would Jesus Do?" bracelet, seemed for many years to live a charmed life. He was a big-league ballplayer who enjoyed his best season after being traded to the Tigers, the team he'd rooted for as a youth. He had a productive ten-year career, winning two world championships as a member of one of the greatest teams in baseball history, the New York Yankees of the late 1990s. Curtis hit 2 home runs in the 1999 World Series—including a walk-off homer in Game Three—to help the Yankees beat the Atlanta Braves.

Then came the downfall.

Chad David Curtis was born on November 6, 1968, in Marion, Indiana, but was raised in Middleville, a village in western Michigan about twenty miles southeast of Grand Rapids. The community, situated near two large state game areas, attracts a fair number of hunters during deer season.

By the time Curtis entered high school, his father had moved his family to Benson, Arizona, for a teaching job there. Curtis played baseball and junior varsity football at Benson High School but was kicked off the school's basketball team for constantly fighting with teammates, an issue that would follow him throughout his career.

Curtis was a solid high school athlete, but he got no college scholarship offers. He attended Yavapai Community College in Prescott, Arizona, and successfully tried out for the baseball team, hitting .360 with 30 runs batted in during his first season. The following year, he transferred to Cochise Community College, where he hit .407 with 15 homers and 71 RBI.

The lofty averages racked up at small colleges failed to attract full scholarship offers from any major universities. His best choices were a quarter-scholarship from the University of Arizona and a full ride at Grand Canyon College. Curtis said he chose the latter because blue-chip prospect Tim Salmon attended Grand Canyon College. Curtis figured there'd be a lot of scouts at those games, giving him the best chance to be signed.

The plan worked. Salmon attracted dozens of scouts every game, and he didn't disappoint, hitting .356 with 19 homers and 68 RBI. The California Angels picked him in the third round of the 1989 draft.

Curtis was even better, posting a .369 batting average with 19 home runs, 83 RBI and 36 stolen bases. But, perhaps put off by his size, nobody drafted him until the Angels finally took him in the forty-fifth round.

Curtis spent three years in the minor leagues. After he hit .316 and stole 46 bases for the Edmonton Trappers in the Pacific Coast League, the Angels called him up to start the 1992 season as the fourth outfielder. He didn't sit on the bench for long; he got into 139 games in his rookie season, hitting .259 with a .341 on-base percentage and 46 stolen bases.

His numbers were even better the following year: a .285 batting average, .361 on-base percentage and 48 steals. But he was also gaining a reputation for being a problem in the clubhouse. Angel batting coach and Hall-of-Famer Rod Carew called Curtis "un-coachable" after the two clashed.

Curtis also annoyed teammates by imposing his morality on them in the locker room. He'd turn off music containing lyrics he considered offensive and shut off the clubhouse television set while his fellow players were watching *The Jerry Springer Show* or other programs he deemed inappropriate.

His attitude likely contributed to Curtis playing for six teams in ten years. During spring training in 1995, two weeks before the season opener, the Tigers swapped popular, versatile infielder Tony Phillips to the Angels for Curtis.

The deal immediately paid dividends for Detroit. Curtis, who was inserted into the leadoff spot, posted career highs in five offensive categories, including batting average (.268), home runs (21) and plate appearances (670), the latter leading the American League.

But the hometown boy didn't stay home for long. The Tigers traded Curtis to the Los Angeles Dodgers for two middling pitching prospects at the trading deadline on July 31, 1996, as part of a salary dump. On the same day, the Tigers swapped Cecil Fielder to the Yankees for an over-the-hill Ruben Sierra and a nondescript pitcher.

Curtis bounced around the majors for a few years with stops in Cleveland and Texas, but his moment of glory came in pinstripes, when he blasted a tenth-inning walk-off homer to lead the Yankees to a win in Game Three of the 1999 World Series.

He retired following the 2001 season and began working with young athletes in western Michigan. After earning a teaching certificate, he took a job as a physical education teacher and coach at Caledonia High School for two years before being named athletic director at Northpointe Christian High School. Shortly into the school year in 2009, Curtis was fired. It's unknown why he was let go, since personnel records from the private school are not available.

The ex-ballplayer then took a job at Lakewood High School in Lake Odessa, where Curtis resided. He served as a substitute teacher and weight-room volunteer and would later be named head football coach.

In May 2012, Curtis resigned after several female students accused him of touching them inappropriately. He was charged with five counts of criminal sexual conduct, and in June 2012, he was bound over for trial. Two months later, a sixth sexual assault charge was levied against him.

Testimony during the Barry County Circuit Court trial was damning.

One of the victims, a fifteen-year-old girl named Kayla, testified that a family friend had told her to talk to Curtis if she wanted to get in shape for sports. She spoke to the ex-ballplayer, who set up a workout regimen for her. He agreed to open the gym early for Kayla and her brother.

There were no reported problems until the following summer, when Kayla, who was in between her sophomore and junior years at Lakewood, started training for the cross-country team. She started having problems with her hip flexors, and Curtis offered to help her with manual hip exercises, in the presence of his two daughters in the weight room.

Kayla said the exercises were uneventful for a few weeks. Then, she said, Curtis changed the training location to a windowless room in the school's basement. Also, the latest rounds of sessions were being held without Curtis's daughters present.

Kayla testified that the workouts started making her feel uncomfortable. "He'd touch all around my leg, and he'd touch up near my hip bones and inside of my hip bones," she testified. "I'm uncomfortable, but I don't say anything because in my head I'm going through all the talks that he had talked in class, and how he was such a Christian guy. And so I was like don't, you know, don't think there's something happening here that's not. You know, don't offend him."

Kayla said one day Curtis told her to lie on the trainer's table on her stomach and then began massaging her hands before working his way up to her shoulders. She said he told her, "relax, you're too tense," before removing her shirt, leaving her in a sports bra. He then flipped her on her back and massaged her stomach.

Then, Kayla said, Curtis climbed onto the table and straddled her. "Once again I tell myself, 'Well, he's just trying to have a better angle at massaging my abdomen,'" Kayla testified.

Kayla said Curtis asked: "Are you sure you're okay with this?"

The teen didn't stop him, so Kayla said Curtis removed her bra and massaged her bare breasts. "I try to rationalize why he could think that it was OK to do that," she testified. "I was trying to figure out how it could better me as an athlete, because that was the idea of this massage. And I couldn't figure out like how that could make sense. And I wanted to say something, but I couldn't even open my mouth to say anything."

Kayla said Curtis finished the breast massage and then touched her crotch before wrapping up the session.

The next day, according to the teen, Curtis approached her and said: "Kayla, we need to talk. Something went terribly wrong." Then, she said, he told her "it was a lesson for the two of us. [Curtis said he had] an angel on one shoulder and a devil on the other. He said it was an inner struggle and he needed to take these thoughts captive and just throw them out."

Kayla said she accepted his apology and resumed training. She said he removed her clothes, including her bra, a second time. She said she looked in his eyes. "They looked animalistic, or demonic," she said.

Then, she said, Curtis kissed her breast as he penetrated her vagina with his finger. She said she pushed him away and told him "no."

Kayla said Curtis then begged her not to tell anyone. "He's like, 'if you go to the police'…he's like, 'I will lose my job.…[My wife] will be extremely hurt, and I probably won't see my kids again,'" she testified. "[He said], 'but Kayla, that's not your fault. I made this decision, and these are the consequences I have to deal with. If that's what you need to do, go to the police, then that's what you need to do.'"

Then Curtis asked the girl to pray with him, Kayla said. They did, and he promised to never touch her inappropriately again. But before she walked away, she said he asked her, "Did you enjoy any of that?"

She said she didn't, "and he turns it into a lesson, and he goes, 'Well, good, now I know that if you ever get into a situation with a boy, you'll be able to make an excuse or go home,' or something like that," Kayla testified.

Kayla said she stopped going to the basement trainer's room after that, although she continued hanging out with Curtis's daughter. "I decided I was going to pretend," she testified. "And if I was going to make this commitment to pretend like nothing happened, then I had to make it look like nothing changed much."

Two other girls, Jessica and Alexis, took the witness stand during Curtis's trial and told similar stories. A male student, Kaleb, also testified, saying Curtis seemed to take an unusual interest in Jessica, a fifteen-year-old sophomore. Curry said Curtis would regularly pull her out of gym class to take her to the basement trainer's room to work with her. Kaleb claimed the coach told him Jessica had a "nice athletic butt."

"I kind of feel like he paid more attention to Jessica…than any other person in there," Kaleb testified. "[The training room sessions were] kind of suspicious. It didn't seem right."

According to telephone records presented in court, and testimony, Curtis and Jessica shared 115 text messages during a two-month period in 2012. Although most of the messages dealt with mundane training issues, Curtis often asked the girl about her boyfriend, telling her she was too good for him and that she was attractive.

Jessica said she began having feelings for her trainer. She texted him, "I would have a thing for you."

Curtis texted back: "I don't want to see my kids in jail."

The next day, Jessica testified: "He told me he didn't think that we should text anymore because he didn't want his wife to be mad."

"I had a crush on him, but it wasn't anything that I would ever take," Jessica said.

Then, in August 2011, Jessica said she felt pain in her ribs and asked Curtis to wrap the area with a bandage. She said he asked her to lift her bra, exposing her breast, and asked, "Is this okay?"

Jessica said she didn't reply negatively, so Curtis lifted her bra completely, exposing her breasts. She said he wrapped her ribs and then she left the training room to attend volleyball practice.

After that, Jessica said Curtis repeatedly pulled her out of class to massage her. One day, she said he pulled her sweatpants down, moved her underwear to the side and began massaging her buttocks.

"I wasn't so much scared," Jessica testified. "I was uncomfortable. But I trusted he was doing his job."

Alexis, who was a fifteen-year-old freshman when she first encountered Curtis, said she had a similar experience with the ex-major-leaguer. She said Curtis approached her after she'd injured her knee while sledding, claiming he could help her heal faster. She said she turned him down at first but that he wouldn't take no for an answer. Alexis said she finally agreed to let him treat her, "because I was sick of him asking me," she testified.

In the basement trainer's room, Alexis said Curtis rubbed her knee before working his way up to her crotch. She said he turned her onto her stomach and rubbed her buttocks with both hands.

Alexis said Curtis took her down to the trainer's room again the next day and repeated the touching. She said he was touching her butt when a fellow student unlocked the door to fetch something for a teacher. Alexis said she saw panic on Curtis's face.

"I was uncomfortable the whole time, but when I saw his reaction, that's when I knew that something was wrong," she testified.

Alexis said she told the police about the touching the following day. Curtis was suspended while the investigation commenced.

Alexis said she got backlash from fellow students and coaches for telling on Curtis. Many Lake Odessa residents openly supported Curtis and questioned the girls' motives. "I no longer enjoy going to school," Alexis testified. "I hear the gossip and I had to quit volleyball because [team tryouts] were the same week as the trial, and the coaches didn't show support for my decision. I got really depressed because like everyone started treating me differently [after she told of the abuse]."

On August 16, 2013, a Barry County jury deliberated for less than three hours before finding Curtis guilty on six counts of criminal sexual conduct.

Curtis didn't take the stand during the weeklong trial but gave a rambling, fifty-minute speech during his sentencing hearing, in which he said the victims were lying and that they had propositioned him. One of the girls left the courtroom while Curtis was discussing her.

"I hope that's hard for her," Curtis said as the victim walked out of the room, "and I hope that from that hardness she says what is true.

"I think this whole thing is an unfortunate situation where the whole truth has not been told," Curtis said. "I believe [the victim] and I could write a book someday and it would have a positive impact on a whole lot of people."

After Curtis's sentencing statement, Barry County prosecutor Julie Nakfoor Pratt said: "That was the most selfish, self-serving, victim-blaming statement I've heard in my career as a prosecutor. It speaks volumes about his character, or lack thereof."

Barry County Circuit Court judge Amy McDowell sentenced Curtis to seven to fifteen years in prison.

In the aftermath of the sentencing, residents of Lake Odessa said the Curtis case has caused a rift around town. His victims say they were bullied in the school hallways and on social media by fellow students who supported Curtis and insisted the girls were lying. The victims filed twenty-eight harassment complaints with the school district between Curtis's arrest in 2012 and his conviction in 2013. One of the girls said the abuse became too much and that she eventually transferred to another school district.

In 2014, GQ magazine named Curtis No. 5 on its list "The 25 Biggest Sleazebags in Sports."

"The imprisoned ex-outfielder molested a 15-year-old girl and then told the girl that they should write a book together to prevent future grown men from being seduced by 15-year-old girls," the magazine said.

HOURS BEFORE THE TIGERS' 2014 home opener against the Kansas City Royals, a group of Detroit Tigers were partying at the popular 5th Avenue bar in Royal Oak, a Detroit suburb, when relief pitcher Evan Reed struck up a conversation with a forty-five-year-old woman.

When Reed began that chance conversation, he was an up-and-coming fireballing relief pitcher. By the time the dust settled, his career was over and his name would be associated with a sex crime.

The woman, whose name is being omitted because she's a sexual assault victim, said she and a friend went to the 5th Avenue on March 30, 2014, and that Reed, who was sitting with three other Detroit Tigers, called the woman to his table. The woman said Reed, twenty-eight, lied and told her he was forty-one years old. She claimed she didn't know he was a baseball player. "He didn't seem to fit the profile," she testified in court.

The woman said she was an avid Tiger fan who had planned to go to Opening Day the next day. She painted her fingernails with the Tiger logo, she said.

She said she drank two vodka and tonics and then had a third drink, which she left on her table while she and Reed danced. When she returned, she said she took a sip and that the drink tasted sour.

Reed and the woman left the bar and took a cab to the MotorCity Casino hotel. Surveillance video from the casino showed the woman stumbling and falling as she exited the taxi. Reed eventually picked her up and carried her for several feet.

The woman said she didn't remember much about that night, but the next morning, she said she awoke in Room 621 feeling disoriented. She said she stumbled into the shower, where Reed joined her and, she said, raped her. The woman said she told Reed to stop but that he didn't comply. After the assault, she said she went back to the hotel bed and tried to go to sleep but that Reed forced himself on her again. When she refused, she claims Reed told her to go home.

Four months after the incident, on July 30, 2014, Reed was charged with two counts of third-degree criminal sexual conduct.

Following Reed's preliminary examination in Detroit's Thirty-Sixth District Court, Judge Kenneth King dismissed the rape charges, saying the alleged victim was not credible. The judge noted how the woman's story had changed several times during her testimony.

One inconsistency was that the woman first claimed she didn't know she was with ballplayers in the bar, despite texting a friend, "I'm sitting with Tigers, dummy!" She later said she thought some of the men were baseball players, but not Reed.

King didn't buy her story. "I don't believe the alleged victim when she says she didn't know who these people were," King said. "She said she didn't know they were Tigers until two days later…why are you being less than truthful?"

King also pointed out that the woman claimed to be disoriented and barely able to stand when she left Reed's hotel room, but video showed her walking down six flights of stairs in high heels without wobbling. King also noted that she walked past a hotel employee in the hallway and a Detroit police car immediately upon exiting the hotel but didn't ask for help.

Following King's decision to dismiss the charges, Reed appeared relieved as he spoke to reporters outside the courthouse. "I have my life back," he said. "This nightmare has gone on longer than it should have. Now I can concentrate on baseball and hopefully pitch for the Tigers again."

Reed, who had been demoted to the minor leagues, was called up to the Tigers in August 2014, about a week after his charges were dismissed. However, his comeback would be short-lived.

Wayne County prosecutors appealed Judge King's ruling, and in November 2014, Wayne County circuit judge Michael Callahan ordered Reed bound over for trial on the criminal sexual conduct charges, ruling that King had abused his discretion in dismissing the case.

"My task today isn't to determine the guilt or innocence of Mr. Reed," Callahan said after binding the case over for trial. "My sole decision is whether or not the magistrate below abused his discretion in refusing to bind the defendant over on the charges."

On July 17, 2015, Reed pleaded no contest to a misdemeanor aggravated assault charge. He was sentenced to one year of probation.

Reed, once a decent pitching prospect whose fastball topped out at ninety-seven miles per hour, never pitched in the major leagues again after the 2014 season.

THROUGH THE YEARS, THE Tigers have had their share of infamous drunkards. Hall of Fame slugger Harry Heilmann, a heavy boozer, once reportedly was inebriated when he drove his car down the steps of a basement speakeasy, pulled up to the bar and ordered a drink. Pitcher Tommy Bridges, the hero of the Tigers' first world championship of 1935, reportedly wound up a skid row bum after he retired.

The names of Tiger ballplayers occasionally show up in Detroit-area court drunk-driving dockets. The perpetrators whose cases garnered the most media attention were former pitcher and broadcaster Lary Sorensen and heavy-hitting infielder Miguel Cabrera.

Sorensen was one of the best pitchers to ever come out of Michigan. He starred at Mount Clemens L'Anse Creuse High School and pitched for the University of Michigan before being selected by the Milwaukee Brewers in the eighth round of the 1976 amateur draft.

The lanky pitcher was in the major leagues by age twenty-one and was an All-Star the following year. But he drank himself out of baseball by age thirty-two. Then, things got worse.

Sorensen's first drunk-driving conviction came in 1992, four years after he'd retired from baseball. Ten months later, he was arrested for the same offense.

He was given a second chance in 1995, when he was named color analyst on Detroit Tiger radio broadcasts with lead announcer Frank Beckmann. Sorensen left the job in June 1998 for undisclosed personal reasons.

There were more drunk-driving arrests—two in 1999, and one apiece in 2003 and 2004.

Following the 2004 conviction, Sorensen was sentenced to from twenty-three to sixty months in prison. After his release, he took a job at a McDonald's restaurant in Roseville, Michigan, for three months while also working at a storage facility in nearby St. Clair Shores. The local media pounced on the story of a former All-Star ballplayer flipping burgers and renting out lockers for minimum wage.

In 2008, Sorensen was arrested a seventh time for drunk driving. He had driven his car into a ditch near 23 Mile Road in Chesterfield Township, Michigan, where an officer found him slumped over the steering wheel, unconscious. His blood alcohol content was .48—six times the legal limit.

Because there was no key in the ignition, Macomb County prosecutors didn't file drunk-driving charges, although a judge sent him back to prison for violating probation from his earlier convictions.

Sorensen was released from prison in 2009 but continued drinking heavily for the next five years, he said.

Around 2014, the Michigan native says he started to turn his life around. He returned to the broadcast booth that year, doing color commentary for Wake Forest University baseball radio broadcasts and television color commentary for the Winston-Salem Dash, a Chicago White Sox minor-league club. In 2017, Sorensen began doing radio color commentary for Wake Forest's football team.

In 2018, Sorensen told *Detroit News* columnist Neal Rubin he hadn't had a drink in more than four years.

Sorensen told Rubin he'd recently had a medical checkup and that he wrote down a list of bad things he'd done in his life. He said the doctor told him if he'd done half the things he'd written down, he was a miracle of modern medicine.

"Doc," Sorensen replied, "I only wrote down half of it because I was embarrassed."

CABRERA WAS THE BEST hitter on the planet when he had his drunken run-ins with the law, so they got widespread media attention. His high-profile drunk-driving arrest was part of a series of embarrassments for the native Venezuelan.

Cabrera came to the Tigers before the 2008 season in one of the best trades in team history that saw Detroit swap blue-chip prospects outfielder Cameron Maybin and pitcher Andrew Miller, along with other minor leaguers, for Cabrera and pitcher Dontrelle Willis. Although Willis was a bust who had major control problems and Miller became a top relief pitcher, the trade was still a huge win for the Tigers, with Cabrera blossoming into one of the best hitters in baseball history.

Trouble started the year after his arrival, as the 2009 season wound down with the Tigers in the thick of the American League Central race. On October 2, with only two games left in the season, Cabrera joined a group of unidentified Chicago White Sox players at the five-star Townsend Hotel in Birmingham, a tony Detroit suburb. The ballplayers reportedly drank until dawn. A few hours later, in a crucial game against the White Sox, Cabrera went 0 for 4.

That night, a Saturday, Cabrera again reportedly got drunk in the Townsend Hotel and was given a ride home by the doorman. Once home, the slugger got into a fight with his wife, Rosangel Cabrera, who called police from an upstairs bedroom. She claimed her husband struck her after she complained about him talking loudly on his cell phone call and waking up their four-year-old daughter.

"I need help please," Rosangel said on the 911 call as she sobbed.

Police later escorted Miguel Cabrera to the Birmingham police station. The ballplayer was uncooperative, police officials said. Before he was released at about 7:30 a.m. to the custody of Tigers team president/general manager Dave Dombrowski, police administered a breathalyzer test. He registered a blood alcohol content of 0.26 percent, or more than three times the limit for motorists; but since he wasn't driving, police didn't charge him.

That day, the Tigers played the Minnesota Twins in a one-game playoff to determine which team would continue in the postseason. Cabrera hit a two-run home run in the third inning to open the scoring, but the Tigers lost, 6–5, in twelve innings.

Cabrera stayed out of trouble for years. Then, on February 16, 2011, he had another high-profile, alcohol-related run-in with the law in which he dared a cop to kill him and swigged a bottle of scotch in front of officers while a dashboard camera rolled.

Hours before his arrest in St. Lucie County, Florida, Cabrera threatened to kill a restaurant manager and customers, according to reports released by police. Fletcher Nail, manager of the Cowboys Bar-B-Q & Steak Co. in Fort Pierce, told police that Cabrera walked into the restaurant at 10:15 p.m. and was informed it was about to close. Cabrera ignored the manager, walked up to a table full of people and began chatting with them, Nail said.

Nail told police he asked the people at the table whether they knew Cabrera, and they said they didn't. Nail again asked Cabrera to leave, he told police.

"You don't know me," Cabrera told Nail, according to police reports.

"No, sir, I do not," Nail responded before opening the door and telling Cabrera to leave. The restaurant manager said the ballplayer leaned in close to Nail and said, "I will kill you." He then patted a bag on his shoulder and threatened to blow up the restaurant, Nail told police.

Cabrera left the restaurant, got into his Jaguar Land Rover and started to drive away as he cursed at the manager and a customer who had written down his license plate number, Nail told police. The customer, Kyle Patterson, an agent with the Florida Fish and Wildlife Conservation Commission, told police that Cabrera threatened him and Nail by saying, "He had a gun in his bag for us."

Just before 11:00 p.m., Cabrera was stopped by a St. Lucie County sheriff's deputy on Florida Highway 70. Deputy Michael Muller said smoke was coming from the engine. It was later determined that the heater hose had come loose, causing the engine to overheat.

Muller told Cabrera to stay in his vehicle, but the ballplayer exited the SUV, "stumbling and slurring his speech," according to police reports and video of the traffic stop. When the cop asked if there was anyone else in the vehicle, Cabrera said, "I'll [expletive] kill him. I'll [expletive] shoot him right now."

The slugger then grabbed a fifth of James Buchanan scotch whiskey and guzzled from it before flipping the bird to the deputy.

Another cop, a Florida highway patrol trooper, arrived and ordered Cabrera to kneel on the ground. Instead, Cabrera stumbled onto the highway and walked around in circles.

"Do you know who I am?" Cabrera asked. "I'm Miguel Cabrera. I play for the Detroit Tigers. You don't know my family."

The trooper again ordered Cabrera to the ground, but he still didn't comply. "Shoot me. Kill me," Cabrera said to the cop. The trooper then pulled out his Taser and ordered Cabrera to get out of the road. The player finally complied. He was handcuffed and taken into custody.

Cabrera pleaded no contest to a charge of drunken driving and was sentenced to one year of probation and fifty hours of community service.

UGUETH URTAÍN URBINA HOLDS two distinctions: He's the only player in baseball history with the initials U.U.U., and he's the only player in history to have his career cut short because he tried to slash men with a machete and set them on fire.

Urbina, a native of Venezuela, enjoyed a solid eleven-year major-league career as a relief pitcher. The two-time All-Star led the National League in saves with 41 in 1999 and helped the Florida Marlins beat the New York Yankees to win the 2003 World Series. He wound up his career with 237 saves, 814 strikeouts and a 3.45 ERA after playing for the Montreal Expos, Boston Red Sox, Texas Rangers, Marlins, Tigers and Philadelphia Phillies.

Urbina began his career with the Expos in 1995. In March 2004, he signed with the Tigers as a free agent. Detroit management said they originally envisioned Urbina to be the eighth-inning setup man as part of what team officials called the "FUP" plan —Kyle Farnsworth pitching the seventh inning, Urbina handling the eighth and recently signed free agent Troy Percival closing. But when Percival got hurt, Urbina was handed the closer's job. He notched 21 saves with a 4.50 ERA.

That September, Urbina left the team to fly to his native Venezuela, where his mother had been kidnapped. According to officials, four men disguised as police officers accosted Maura Villareal from a home owned by her ballplayer son. The kidnappers demanded $6 million in ransom.

The ordeal dragged on for five months, until February 18, 2005, when members of a Venezuelan police anti-kidnapping unit stormed a mountain camp and rescued the woman. One of the abductors was killed, but Urbina's mother was not hurt.

Urbina got off to a good start in the 2005 season, with 9 saves and a 2.63 ERA. Then, on June 8, the Tigers traded him to Philadelphia for second baseman Placido Polanco. Urbina got into 56 games with the Phillies, but his season soured as he posted a 4.13 ERA in the season's final three months.

About a month after the 2005 season ended, on November 7, Urbina attended a welcome-home party at his mother's ranch. He went out to eat and returned to the home at about 2:00 a.m. Farmworkers told police that Urbina began asking about a gun that was missing. Then, Urbina and three friends rounded up all the workers, attacked them with a machete and poured gasoline and paint thinner on them and set them on fire.

"Urbina was the one commanding the whole thing," victim Bernardo Navarros, whose upper torso was sliced by the machete, told Knight-Ridder Newspapers.

Urbina's attorney insisted that the men were trying to steal the ballplayer's fortune. They also pointed out that Urbina was on high alert after his mother had been kidnapped. In addition, his father had been killed in 1994 by men who were trying to steal a truck the pitcher had bought him.

The defense's tactics didn't work; Urbina was found guilty and sentenced in 2007 to fourteen years in prison. However, in December 2012, after serving only five and a half years of his sentence, Urbina was released for good behavior, Venezuelan officials said.

6

FROM THE CELLBLOCK
TO THE CORNER

Gates Brown was one of the best pinch hitters in baseball history. Ron LeFlore was one of the most exciting players of the late 1970s. Both men's considerable talents were languishing behind bars before they traded in their prison garb for the Olde English *D*.

The baseball establishment wasn't always welcoming to ex-cons. In 1935, Edwin "Alabama" Pitts was released from Sing Sing Prison in upstate New York after serving six years for robbery. Sing Sing had a legendary baseball team that had once played the New York Yankees, and Pitts was a prison-yard star. When he was paroled, the Albany Senators of the International League offered him a minor-league contract for $200 a month, but IL officials blocked the transaction. The case was appealed to baseball commissioner Kenesaw Mountain Landis, who overturned the decision and allowed Pitts to play. The ex-convict bounced around the minors for a few years and later died in a bar fight.

Landis's decision paved the way for the Tigers in 1959 to sign a musclebound, hard-hitting catcher who was serving time or at the Ohio State Reformatory for breaking into a theater.

William James "Gates" Brown was born in Crestline, Ohio, on May 2, 1939, the same day fabled Yankee first baseman Lou Gehrig ended his consecutive games streak in Detroit at 2,130 games.

Contrary to myth, Brown didn't get his nickname because he'd been locked behind prison gates. "My mother started calling me Gates when I was small," he told the *Detroit Free Press*. "I still don't know where she got it. But the name stuck."

Brown's talent for hitting a baseball emerged early. At age ten, he annoyed his American Legion coach by purposely hitting baseballs into a creek beyond the playing grounds.

"The devil just came out in me," he told the *Free Press*. "Guys would line up to protect the ball from the creek. I'd hit it and everyone would start running to keep it from going in that stinky, oily water."

Brown was a star in both baseball and football at Crestline High School. Jack Harbaugh, a college football player and coach, father of University of Michigan football coach Jim Harbaugh and a Crestline alumnus, called Brown the greatest running back in school history. Colleges were sniffing around, ready to offer scholarships.

But Brown was also a troublemaker. In an oft-repeated quote that was printed in numerous Detroit Tiger books and yearbooks, when asked what subjects he took in high school, Brown replied, "I took a little English, a little math, some science, a few hubcaps and some wheel covers."

On February 7, 1958, when Brown was eighteen and about to start his senior year in high school, he and a gang of kids broke into the Crest Theater and stole $400. Brown was the only one of his crew to get arrested.

"That made me bitter," he told former catcher and announcer Joe Garagiola in a two-part episode of *The Baseball World of Joe Garagiola* television show. "I thought society had done me a great injustice."

Brown was convicted of breaking and entering and sent to the Ohio State Reformatory, a haunting, Romanesque Revival prison built in 1886 that was featured in the movie *The Shawshank Redemption*.

"That first night, when I lay down to go to sleep, I cried," he told Garagiola. "Until you actually go through it, you have no idea what it's like. At 4:30 or 5, you're locked up until the next morning. In the spring and summer, the sun is shining, the birds are singing and you keep asking yourself, 'Why me?'"

Amid the misery, there were opportunities to play ball. Brown caught on the prison team, which played once a week against semipro teams around Ohio. The reformatory's athletic director, Chuck Yarman, was wowed by Brown's ability to hit a baseball and contacted the Cleveland Indians, Chicago White Sox and the Tigers.

Each team sent scouts to the prison to watch Brown play. The White Sox scout saw one game and passed. But the Indians and Tigers were impressed. In the game Tiger scout Pat Mullin watched, Brown hit two home runs over the prison wall.

"They made bids and finally, they both said they were going to offer me the same thing, $7,000, and I was to choose which team I wanted to play with," Brown told Garagiola.

The man teammates would affectionately call "The Gator" chose the Tigers. "There were no black players in Detroit at the time," he told the *Detroit News*. "I felt they were looking for one, and that I'd have a better chance of making the big leagues with them."

With the help of Tiger management, Brown was released early from the prison after serving twenty-two months. In the fall of 1959, he signed his first professional baseball contract that included a $7,000 bonus. He was assigned to the Duluth-Superior Dukes, the Tigers' Class A farm team in the Northern League.

Mullin, the scout who signed Brown, suggested he give up catching and become an outfielder. The move paid off; in 1960, his first year in pro ball and still on probation, Brown hit .293 with 10 homers and a .392 on-base percentage. He also led the Northern League with 13 triples and finished second with 30 stolen bases and 104 runs scored.

In 1961, Brown was promoted to the Durham Bulls in the Carolina League, a Class B team. He said he was greeted with racist vitriol from the southern crowds.

"It was tough just being a Negro down there," he told the *Sporting News*. "They still used the N-word down there, you know?"

Brown said fans also heckled him about his criminal history. "They called me all the names: 'Con,' 'Jailbird,' the whole thing," he told the *Sporting News*. "They were pretty vicious. Some of the guys wanted to go up into the stands after those people, but I told them to just let it lay. It made me do better. It made me try harder. I decided that they could beat me physically, but no way were they going to beat me mentally. And do you know something? I hit the ball hard that season and led the league in hitting."

Brown led the Carolina League that year with a .324 average, and Brown said the fans who'd been riding him earlier in the year had warmed to him by season's end. "By the end of the year, they were all on my side," he told the *Sporting News*.

The following season brought another promotion, this time to the AA Denver Bears in the American Association. Brown hit .300 in 1962. He started the 1963 season with the AAA Syracuse Chiefs in the International League, although he played only sixty games until, on June 17, he was called up to the major-league club.

Brown made his major-league debut for the Tigers two days later against the Boston Red Sox at Fenway Park. Boston was leading 4–1 in the fifth inning when manager Charlie Dresson told Brown to pinch-hit for pitcher Don Mossi. Brown hit a four-hundred-foot homer off Red Sox pitcher Bob Hefner, who was making his first major-league start. The Gator's home run didn't help; the Tigers lost, 9–2, to drop their ninth straight game.

Brown would get into fifty-five games with the Tigers that season, hitting .268 with 2 homers and a .768 on-base percentage plus slugging percentage (OPS).

He was in the major leagues to stay. During his first five years with the Tigers, he averaged .259, 7 home runs and a .755 OPS.

Then came the magical 1968 season, when an inspirational Tiger team defied the odds and won the World Series, while Brown turned in arguably the greatest season by a pinch hitter in baseball history. Overall, counting both pinch-hitting and games he started, Brown went 34 for 92 for a .370 average, posting a .442 on-base percentage, a .685 slugging percentage and a 1.127 OPS. He struck out just four times.

When called on to pinch-hit, Brown was even better, hitting .450 in 39 at bats, with 3 home runs and 9 extra-base hits while fanning only once.

The heroics started in the season's second game, when Tiger manager Mayo Smith called on Brown to hit for relief pitcher Jon Warden to lead off the ninth inning with the game tied, 2–2. In his first at bat of the season, Brown blasted Red Sox pitcher John Wyatt's second pitch into the right-field upper deck, and the Tigers won.

Brown was a deep, philosophical man who mentored young ballplayers and became an outspoken critic of how African Americans were treated by the baseball establishment. But he also was a bit of a goofball, and his flub on August 7, 1968, is the stuff of legend.

According to the oft-told story, Brown, as usual, wasn't in the starting lineup in the home game against the Cleveland Indians, so he decided to sneak a couple of hot dogs from the clubhouse. The manager picked that unfortunate time to tell Brown to pinch-hit—so Brown stuffed the hot dogs in his jersey to hide them from the skipper.

"I always wanted to get a hit every time I went to the plate," he told the *Sporting News*. "But this was one time I didn't want to get a hit. I'll be damned if I didn't smack one in the gap and I had to slide into second—head first, no less. I was safe with a double. But when I stood up, I had mustard and ketchup and smashed hot dogs and buns all over me. The fielders took one look at me, turned their backs and damned near busted a gut laughing at me. My teammates in the dugout went crazy."

Smith fined Brown $100 and reportedly asked him, "What the hell were you doing eating on the bench in the first place?"

Brown says he replied honestly, "I was hungry."

Brown continued his career as a pinch hitter, although he often expressed a desire to start more. When the designated hitter rule was adopted by the American League in 1973, Brown became the primary DH against right-handed pitchers, but by then he was past his prime.

After thirteen seasons, all with Detroit, Brown retired after the 1975 campaign. He holds American League records for most lifetime pinch-hit at bats, (414), most pinch hits (107) and most pinch-hit home runs (16).

The Gator stayed with the Tiger organization, signing on as a scout immediately after retiring and then serving as hitting coach from 1978 until he quit following the 1984 season.

Brown's post-baseball affairs were rocky. In 1991, he invested in Ben G Industries, a plastics molding company that became mired in allegations that the previous owners had stolen $458,000 before selling the firm to Brown's investment group. The Internal Revenue Service investigated and found that Brown hadn't paid taxes his first two years of owning the company. The IRS filed a civil suit against Brown seeking $61,000. That wasn't Brown's first flap with the IRS; a few months before the Ben G trial started, Brown and his wife, Norma, were charged with underpaying their personal taxes from 1992 to 1997 and were ordered to pay more than $36,000 in back taxes and penalties.

The big man's health began to deteriorate. He contracted diabetes and was hospitalized for the last weeks of his life. On September 27, 2013, Brown died of a heart attack. He was seventy-four.

Brown made a mistake early in life, and, his tax issues notwithstanding, he never again ran afoul of the law. He served for years as a positive role model for younger Tiger players and fans.

The second player the Tigers signed out of prison was even more talented. When Detroit signed him in July 1973, Brown expressed hope the new guy would turn his life around like he had. "This may be his last go-round in life, like it was with myself," Brown said. "I was able to take advantage of my opportunity, and I hope he can, too."

The new player certainly made an impact on the field. But unlike Brown, Ron LeFlore couldn't stay out of legal trouble after getting a second chance.

LeFLORE'S TIGER CAREER STARTED with a pack of lies.

When the Tigers signed the speedy outfielder to a contract in July 1973, just hours after he was released from Michigan State Prison in Jackson, the acquisition made national headlines. LeFlore, formerly Inmate no. B-115614, told reporters he was twenty-one and that he'd just served time for an armed robbery he'd committed at age seventeen, a one-time, ill-advised youthful indiscretion.

It was bunk. LeFlore was four years older than he'd claimed. And while it's true he'd been locked up at age seventeen, that was for a different crime than the one for which he was incarcerated when the Tigers signed him. In fact, records showed he'd been sentenced to prison on three separate occasions.

When Tiger management was presented the facts dug up by *Detroit Free Press* reporters three years after LeFlore's signing, general manager Jim Campbell said: "Frankly, it's of no concern to me. I could care less…the only concern I have is that he can play ball."

On that front, Campbell had no worries. For all his shortcomings, LeFlore was a supremely gifted ballplayer.

He was born on June 16, 1948, in Detroit and grew up on the city's east side, which for years has been one of the most violent areas in the country. He was the third of four boys to his parents, John and Georgia LeFlore, who'd moved to Detroit from Memphis in 1943, like millions of other southerners looking for auto-plant jobs. John LeFlore landed such a gig, but because of his alcoholism, he couldn't hold on to it. He bounced from job to job, while John's wife worked as a nurse's aide.

Like many children in his neighborhood, Ron LeFlore learned "the game" early in life. In the book *Breakout: From Prison to the Big Leagues*, the autobiography he coauthored with longtime *Detroit Free Press* sportswriter Jim Hawkins, LeFlore said he embarked early on in a life of crime.

"Our neighborhood was the worst," he said. "It was truly crime-infested. Prostitution, robbery, drugs, murder—everything you could possibly think of was going on in the six or seven block area near where we lived. The favorite pastime of the community was committing crimes; it was the 'in' thing to do.

"Stealing was my specialty," LeFlore said. "As far back as I can remember, I was stealing things and getting away with it.…Every time I went into a store, I would steal something, even if it was just a rubber ball or one of those ten-cent miniature pies, just to show the other kids I could do it. Sometimes I would steal for the thrill of it. I got away with so much stuff that I began to believe I couldn't get caught. Usually everything I did was right out in the open, too. I thought I was the Invisible Man."

LeFlore says he started drinking at eleven and smoked marijuana for the first time two years later. At age fifteen, he began experimenting with hard drugs, eventually working his way up to heroin. LeFlore was first arrested in July 1965 at age seventeen for attempting to break into a safe. He was convicted in January 1966 and sentenced to eighteen months in prison. Records from the Michigan Department of Corrections are incomplete, but state officials said LeFlore probably served his time in a minimum-security facility until he was paroled in July 1967.

It wasn't long before he was behind bars again. In May 1968, police arrested him in Detroit's red-light district, the Cass Corridor. While the reason for his arrest has not survived Detroit police records, the infraction violated his parole, and he was sent to a prison farm for sixteen months.

Four months after his September 1969 parole, LeFlore was arrested yet again, this time for armed robbery. LeFlore said he was coming down from an all-night heroin jag when he cooked up the scheme to rob Dee's Bar, a neighborhood dive across the street from Chrysler's Mack Avenue Stamping Plant on Detroit's east side.

"My best friend, Antoine, a fellow named Leroy and I were hanging around O'Quinn's Poolroom where we lived on Detroit's east side one night in January, 1970—when I suggested we pull a robbery. Just like that," LeFlore recalled in his autobiography. "The three of us had been together the night before, snorting heroin in a dope house across the street, and Antoine and Leroy had spent all their money. They were broke. I had $20 or $30 in my pocket, and we all wanted to get high again, but I wasn't about to spend all my money on dope for them. A robbery seemed like the logical solution."

LeFlore said he didn't need the money, but "I had my image to protect," he said. "By then I had become known as the best thief in the neighborhood, at least among guys my own age, and I was proud of that reputation."

The three powwowed and decided they needed a gun to pull off the caper. According to LeFlore, Antoine offered his .22-caliber rifle. LeFlore would wield the gun during the robbery, "since I was the gutsy one in the group," he said.

The trio decided to rob Dee's, since the bar was known to have lots of money in its register from cashing the Chrysler workers' checks, a common practice in bars near auto plants at the time.

LeFlore and Antoine piled into Leroy's car and drove to the bar on Mack Avenue. There were only a few people inside, so the criminals waited in the alley until they left. "Then the three of us charged in through the back door," LeFlore said.

LeFlore covered the bar owner and his wife while his accomplices emptied the cash registers and floor safe. They put about $35,000 cash and a .38-caliber revolver into a bag and fled out the back door.

According to LeFlore, Leroy hadn't turned on his headlights, and as they escaped from the bar heist, they passed a Detroit police cruiser. The driver of the squad car flashed his lights at Leroy.

"I was sitting in the front seat with the rifle on my lap and I said to Leroy, 'If those mother-fuckers stop us, I'm going to open fire—and you take off,'" LeFlore claimed. "I had my finger on the trigger ready to shoot, but the police were merely blinking their lights to let us know our lights were out."

The robbers stashed the stolen money and gun in a heating vent in Leroy's apartment, and LeFlore says he called a taxi to take him home. "When the cabbie pulled up in front and blew his horn, I looked out and saw police cars all over the street," LeFlore said. "The police who had seen us driving in the vicinity of the robbery driving with our lights out must have taken our license number down, checked and found the car belonged to Leroy."

LeFlore and Antoine dashed to the apartment building's attic to hide. When they got to the top story, they heard the police break into Leroy's first-floor apartment, LeFlore said. He added that he could hear police discussing a robbery. "We knew it wouldn't be long before they'd come searching upstairs," LeFlore said. He decided to pretend he was a resident and try to calmly stroll past the police to make his escape. His plan didn't work; LeFlore claims that as he was walking past Leroy's apartment, his accomplice ratted him out to the police.

LeFlore was convicted of armed robbery in Wayne County Court and sentenced to from five to fifteen years in prison. He was sent to "Jackson" or "Jack-Town"—the street names for the State Prison of Southern Michigan in Jackson.

"Only the worst criminals get sent to Jackson—the murderers, the rapists, the armed robbers," LeFlore said. "I didn't know what to expect. I didn't know whether I was going to be able to survive among all those hardened criminals. I didn't know if I was going to get killed, or raped, or what. All the time I was on the streets, all the things I had done, I was never really scared. But I was scared now."

LeFlore claimed he started playing baseball in prison to get out quicker. "Sports were merely another con, another hustle for me," he said. "I became involved in athletics because the guys who played sports stood a better chance of getting an early parole."

In May 1971, LeFlore tried out for the prison baseball team, and although he claims he'd never hit a hardball with a real baseball bat in his life, he made the cut. The team consisted of a catcher and first baseman who were fellow armed robbers; a keystone combination that was literally murderer's row (the shortstop and second baseman both were convicted killers); and a right fielder who was serving ten to twenty years for rape.

Through baseball, LeFlore met Jimmy Karella, an older inmate doing a stint of from four to twenty years for extortion. Karella recognized LeFlore's jaw-dropping athletic talent and began working with him to develop his raw skills.

Karella's tutelage worked. According to LeFlore, he hit .469 in 1971 and .569 in 1972. A part-time scout for the Milwaukee Brewers saw him play and wrote a letter to his bosses suggesting LeFlore be scouted further, but the Brewer brain trust said they weren't interested.

Karella reached out to his longtime friend Jimmy Butsicaris, co-owner of the Lindell AC bar in downtown Detroit, which was the favorite watering hole for the Tigers and their manager, Billy Martin. The two were best of friends—Butsicaris had been best man at Martin's wedding—and the bar owner convinced the skipper to visit the prison on May 23, 1973, to meet LeFlore.

A few weeks later, state officials granted LeFlore a one-day furlough so he could go to Tiger Stadium for a tryout. "He was hitting balls into the upper deck," Martin told the Associated Press.

Added scout Bill Lajoie: "The raw talent was so good in what we saw that we just had to sign him. But it's a chancy situation. You never know what a kid will do when he gets onto a professional ball field."

The Tigers were about to find out.

LeFlore was paroled on July 2, 1973, and hours later signed a contract with the Tigers calling for $500 a month with a $5,000 signing bonus. He reported to the Clinton (Iowa) Pilots in the Class A Midwest League. The manager was future Tiger skipper Jim Leland, who said he was wary of his new player.

"When I was told I was going to get him, frankly, I didn't know what to expect," Leyland was quoted in LeFlore's autobiography. "I presumed you could have all sorts of problems with a kid on parole. Could he cross state lines with the ball club? Did I have to keep him out of bars and pool halls? What happened if a brawl broke out on the field and he piled on?"

Leyland said his initial fears were unfounded. "As it turned out, I didn't have any problems with Ron at all," he said. "I guess the prison experience must have helped him rather than hurt."

LeFlore appeared in thirty-two games for the Pilots, who would eventually become Midwest League champions. The neophyte ballplayer wound up with a respectable .277 batting average, 1 home run, 8 RBIs and 2 stolen bases.

The Tigers moved LeFlore up a notch to start the 1974 season, sending him to the Class A Lakeland Tigers of the Florida State League. He came into his own, leading the team with a .339 batting average and 42 stolen bases. After ninety-three games, team management sent him to their highest farm club, the Evansville Triplets, a AAA team in the American Association. He didn't fare as well, eking out a .235 batting average.

But when veteran Tiger center fielder Mickey Stanley broke his hand, ending his season, LeFlore was called up to the big leagues. On August 1, 1974, thirteen months after being in prison, LeFlore made his major-league debut against the Brewers, the team that had eschewed him a few years earlier.

It was an inauspicious beginning; LeFlore went 0-for-4 with 3 strikeouts. The next day, he got his first hit and stole two bases. He was on his way.

LeFlore started all but one of the Tigers' final sixty games the rest of the

Ron LeFlore starred for the Tigers from 1974 to 1979, when he was traded because he reportedly couldn't get along with manager Sparky Anderson.

season, finishing at .260 with 2 homers, 13 RBIs and 23 stolen bases. But he was awful in the field, committing 11 errors.

The 1975 campaign was a Jekyll-and-Hyde season. The first half, LeFlore hit .289 with 7 home runs, 28 RBIs and 25 stolen bases. After the All-Star break, he slumped to .206 with 1 homer, 9 RBIs and 3 stolen bases. He finished with a pedestrian .258 batting average and a .302 on-base percentage—woefully low for a leadoff hitter, which was LeFlore's role on the team.

LeFlore's younger brother Gerald, a gangbanger and drug dealer, was killed during the first month of the 1976 season. Gerald LeFlore was shot in the chest during a struggle over a rifle in a house on Detroit's east side.

The tragedy didn't affect LeFlore's playing; the day he learned of the shooting, LeFlore had 3 hits, stole 1 base, scored 1 run and drove in 1 run. It was the early stages of a breakout season. LeFlore started out of the gate hot, with a thirty-game hitting streak, during which he hit a lusty .392. He was the starting center fielder for the American League All-Star team, rapping out a single to lead off the game at Philadelphia's Veterans Stadium.

LeFlore continued his fine season until it ended on September 12, when he ruptured a tendon in his right knee. He finished with a .316 batting average and 58 stolen bases, second in the American League.

The ascension continued for the next three seasons. From 1976 to 1979, LeFlore hit .310 with 243 stolen bases and 429 runs scored, establishing himself as one of the game's greatest players.

But LeFlore couldn't outrun the lure of the streets. He was using drugs and hanging around unsavory characters. When Sparky Anderson, who ran a no-nonsense clubhouse, took over as Tiger manager in June 1979, the writing was on the wall. Although LeFlore had a fine showing in 1979, hitting .300 with 110 runs scored and 78 stolen bases, Anderson was eager to get rid of his center fielder. Two months after the season ended, LeFlore was traded to the Montreal Expos for left-handed pitcher Dan Schatzeder.

Even though Schatzeder had just posted a 10-5 record with a fine 2.83 ERA, Tiger fans were puzzled by the trade of one of the game's biggest stars for a virtually unknown twenty-five-year-old pitching prospect. News of LeFlore's drug use hadn't yet surfaced, and team officials were mum. While Schatzeder never panned out, the Tigers were able to flip him two years later for Larry Herndon, who was a key member of the 1984 world championship team.

Tiger fans could find no silver lining after the 1980 season ended with Schatzeder posting an 11-13 record with a subpar 4.58 ERA, while LeFlore put on one of the greatest base-stealing displays in baseball history. His batting average fell 40 points below his career average to .257, but LeFlore led the National League with 97 stolen bases, good enough at the time for fourth on the all-time single-season stolen base list.

But the Expos weren't enamored of LeFlore's behavior, and team management expressed no interest in him when he became a free agent after the 1980 season. The Chicago White Sox signed him to a multiyear, $9 million contract.

That much money in the hands of a drug addict can be dangerous, and LeFlore's career, which had appeared to be on a Hall of Fame track, went down rapidly. In two seasons with the White Sox, he played only 173 games, hitting just .267 with 64 stolen bases—and his attitude was reportedly worse than his statistics.

LeFlore went into a freefall during the 1982 season. White Sox manager Tony LaRussa, every bit as hard-nosed as Anderson, suspended LeFlore three times during the season. His infractions included falling asleep on the trainer's table during a game, missing flights and practices and, finally getting busted with illegal guns and drugs.

On September 30, 1982, the White Sox were preparing to travel to Minnesota to finish the season with a four-game series against the Twins when they got word their center fielder had been arrested. An informant had tipped off Chicago Police narcotics detectives that LeFlore was buying and using drugs. The police set up surveillance and watched the ballplayer for three months before arresting him in his condominium. Officers confiscated quaaludes and other pills and two unregistered .25-caliber derringers.

"I didn't think I had a substance abuse problem, but I'm quite sure I did," LeFlore would later tell the *Chicago Tribune*. "You never think you have a substance abuse problem, especially if you have the money to pay for it."

On January 16, 1983, the legal troubles took a back seat to tragedy, when six-week-old John Christopher LeFlore, son of Ron and Sara LeFlore, died of sudden infant death syndrome.

Spring training embarked with LeFlore still awaiting trial on the drug and gun charges, and White Sox management grudgingly invited him to camp, hoping to get some return on his hefty salary. But the brass found LeFlore's demeanor hadn't changed. On April 2, the day before the 1983 season opener, the ChiSox released him.

By then, word had spread throughout baseball about LeFlore's negative attitude, and he still had the drug and gun charges hanging over his head. No other team offered him a job.

LeFlore was acquitted in June 1983, when a judge ruled that prosecutors couldn't prove the guns and drugs belonged to him because he shared his condominium with other roommates. LeFlore expressed hope some team would sign him. None did.

In 1984, LeFlore gave an interview with the *Detroit Free Press* in which he insisted he could still help some team. "I would sign a dollar contract if I had to," he said. "I just want a chance. I can still play. I may take out an ad, just to let baseball know where I am."

When Tiger GM Jim Campbell was asked about the possibility of LeFlore being a Tiger again, he was terse. "We have absolutely no interest whatsoever," he said. "That's all I have to say about Ron LeFlore."

The next few years, LeFlore hung around the fringes of baseball, hoping someone would make him an offer. In 1988, he made ends meet by working as a baggage handler for Eastern Airlines while attending former MLB umpire Joe Brinkman's umpiring school in Cocoa, Florida. Top graduates were placed into minor-league jobs after the five-week course was finished, but LeFlore didn't finish high enough in his class to qualify for a position.

LeFlore then played in the Senior Professional Baseball League, but the league disbanded in 1991 after two seasons. He also got a series of coaching and managing gigs with the Frontier League and the Canadian Baseball League, which folded during its first season. The former All-Star often appeared at autograph shows, trying to cash in on his fame.

When Tiger Stadium hosted its final game on September 27, 1999, LeFlore was invited to participate in the festivities. He appeared in uniform during the postgame ceremony and was greeted with cheers from the packed house as he ambled to his former position in center field. Following the game, minutes after he changed into his street clothes in a room under the grandstand, Wayne County sheriff's deputies arrested him for nonpayment of $57,000 in child support.

In May 2007, LeFlore landed in jail again for failing to pay child support; this time, he was $73,000 in arrears. Wayne County sheriff's deputies arrested him at an autograph signing in Mount Clemens, a suburb of Detroit. LeFlore, who had once been worth millions, was charging $4 for his signature before deputies put him in handcuffs and led him out of the Gibraltar Trade Center.

Trouble continued when LeFlore, a lifelong smoker, lost his right leg to arterial vascular disease, which he attributed to his cigarette habit.

Ron LeFlore's life was the subject of a made-for-TV movie, *One in a Million: The Ron LeFlore Story*, which aired on CBS on September 26, 1978, as the star outfielder was wrapping up his finest season. The movie ends on a positive note, with LeVar Burton, the actor who played LeFlore, telling a little boy, "Listen to your folks, not the streets."

Perhaps LeFlore should have taken his doppelganger's advice. In the end, the Ron LeFlore story is a tale of wasted talent. "I made a mark in baseball," LeFlore told the *Chicago Tribune*. "Nobody can take that away from me. But I could have made a much bigger mark in baseball than I did. I could have done so much more."

7

FAN FURY

As Game Three of the 1984 American League Championship Series entered the eighth inning, with a Tiger sweep of the Kansas City Royals and a trip to the World Series imminent, a battalion of Detroit police officers lined up in foul territory in front of the grandstand.

"Something for America to think about…the very sight of it," ABC announcer Howard Cosell lamented, while broadcast partners Al Michaels and Jim Palmer expressed concern that the cops might figure in a play.

Sure enough, Royal second baseman Frank White led off the inning and pulled a foul fly toward the left-field stands—in the exact spot where the officers were lined up. The police scattered as Tiger left fielder Larry Herndon chased the ball, which landed a few rows back. The crowd booed and chanted "Off the field!"

After Tiger third baseman Marty Castillo caught the game's final out, a foul popup from Royal left fielder Darryl Motley that netted the Tigers' first pennant since 1968, the police stood guard in front of the stands, keeping all but a few fans from storming the field. The television camera captured a group of officers tackling a fan as he neared the Tiger dugout. A small group of fans slipped past the officers and dashed into the outfield. The cops chased them, and the crowd booed.

Although it wasn't pretty, the police were able to maintain order.

It was a short-lived victory.

After the Tigers beat the San Diego Padres four games to one to win Detroit's third world championship, fans overwhelmed the cops and staged arguably the most infamous sports riot in U.S. history, giving the city yet another black eye on the national stage.

The behavior, while dreadful, wasn't exactly new. As discussed in earlier chapters, Tiger fans can be a madcap, rowdy lot, and through the years, they've sometimes been downright ugly.

THROUGHOUT TIGER HISTORY, MOST fan rowdiness happened in the bleachers.

The bleachers—and its denizens—were a thorn in the side of Tiger management from the beginning of the franchise, starting with a group of dilapidated wood scaffoldings known as the Wildcat Bleachers, which were erected in back yards and fields that abutted the walls of Boulevard Park and, later, Bennett Park. There were as many as five such dilapidated bleacher sections situated outside Bennett Park.

Tickets for Bennett Park's Wildcat Bleachers, which held about seventy-five to one hundred fans each, cost only a dime—a price that didn't keep the riffraff out. Class resentment surfaced as the "wildcatters," mostly young men,

The "wildcat bleachers" outside Bennett Park was a thorn in the sides of Tiger management and fans with tickets to seats inside the park, who were often spit on and taunted by the rowdy "Wildcatters."

brawled among each other, catcalled female fans and harassed their escorts as they walked to their sanctioned seats inside the ballpark. Sometimes, the wildcatters used the people below, even cops, as target practice.

"The wildcat spectators have been making it a practice to expectorate tobacco on those who pass through the alley while taking a short cut to the grounds," Detroit police patrolman George Green complained to the *Detroit Journal* in 1906. Green told the paper that he showed his tobacco-stained uniform to the police chief as proof of the wildcatters' lack of decorum.

Team owner Frank Navin tried to thwart the nonpaying spectators by erecting strips of canvas along the fences to block their view. Angry fans disrupted games by throwing rotten vegetables and bottles onto the field. Navin finally relented and took down the canvas strips.

The precedent was set. Through the years, Tiger fans became infamous for their habit of voicing their displeasure by throwing things onto the field.

When the Oakland A's came to Detroit in the 1970s, pitcher Paul Lindblad spent time before games scouring the Tiger Stadium outfield with a metal detector. "I've found all kinds of bullets in this ballpark—.22s, .38s, some of them whole, some of them spent," Lindblad told the *Detroit Free Press* in 1975. Other items he found include a screwdriver, old coins, spark plugs, nuts and bolts and rings.

Probably the most talked-about instance involving Tiger fans throwing things onto the playing field was the unrest in the bleachers during Game Seven of the 1934 Fall Classic against the St. Louis Cardinals—one of the most contentious episodes in World Series history.

It happened on October 9, on a windswept, sunny Tuesday afternoon. It had been a tough, physical series up to that point, with profanity flying back and forth between the two benches. The Cardinals, dubbed "The Gashouse Gang," was one of the most rough-and-tumble teams of all time, and the Tigers of that era, featuring such "red-asses" as Mickey Cochrane and Billy Rogell, were no slouches in the scrapping department, either.

As they prepared for the seventh game, the Tigers and their fans were in a dour mood before the first pitch was thrown, because newspaper photos proved that in the previous game umpire Brick Owens had blown a call that likely cost the Tigers a win—and Detroit's first world championship.

Game Seven was effectively over by the third inning, when St. Louis scored seven runs. With the Cardinals' Hall of Fame pitcher Dizzy Dean on the mound throwing bullets, the prospects appeared dim for the home team. The mood among the 40,902 Tiger fans in attendance grew more ominous as each inning passed.

The Cardinal onslaught continued in the sixth inning, when left fielder Joe "Ducky" Medwick hit a bomb to center field. He dashed around the bases and slid into third base in a cloud of dust. Medwick and Tiger third baseman Marv Owen got their feet tangled, and Owen fell to the ground. The crowd, thinking Medwick had been overly aggressive, booed lustily. Medwick would score one of two runs that inning, making the score 9–0 and pushing the bleacher fans past their boiling point.

"When Medwick moved into left field at the end of the inning, the bleacher fans beat him back with a barrage of bottles, oranges, apples and anything else they could lay their hands on," the *Detroit News* observed. "Four times Medwick tried to gain his post, and four times the bleacher boys and girls chased him back."

Manager Mickey Cochrane jogged to the left-field stands and begged the crowd to simmer down. The effort was in vain. The public-address announcer warned over the loudspeaker that the umpires would forfeit the game to the Cardinals if the barrage didn't stop. It didn't stop.

Umpire Harry Geisel, the crew chief, asked Cardinal player-manager Frankie Frisch if he'd be willing to pull Medwick from the game. But Medwick had accumulated 11 hits in the series, one short of the all-time record, and he wanted to keep playing. His manager backed him up, refusing the umpire's request.

So, the ump approached the baseball commissioner, Judge Landis, in his front-row box seat on the first-base line. Landis ordered Medwick out of the game. Newsreel cameras captured the obviously disgusted Cardinal outfielder as he trudged back to his dugout and threw his mitt onto the bench.

Landis later said he had no choice but to pull Medwick from the game. "When it became apparent that the demonstration of the crowd would never terminate, I decided to take action," Landis told the *Minneapolis Tribune*. "I made my decision in order to avert a demonstration leading to possible riot and injury and to protect Medwick from violence....I felt that an even more dangerous outbreak might develop if Medwick continued to play."

Legendary sportswriter Paul Gallico of the *New York Daily News* provided a vivid description of the fans' fury. "I watched the crowd and Medwick and the pelting missiles through my field glasses, and it was a horrifying sight," he wrote. "Every face in the crowd, women and men, was distorted with rage. Mouths were torn wide; open eyes glistened and shone in the sun. All fists were clenched."

St. Louis Cardinal manager–second baseman Frankie Frisch (*left*) and outfielder Joe "Ducky" Medwick (*center*) discuss Commissioner Judge Kenesaw Mountain Landis's decision to remove Medwick from Game Seven of the 1934 World Series after unruly Tiger fans pelted the player with rotten fruit and other projectiles—one of the most infamous incidents in World Series history.

Syndicated columnist Harry Grayson summed up how many observers across the nation felt about the incident, saying it "perhaps was the most disgraceful scene in the annals of the sport."

After the game, fans vented their rage by tearing out home plate.

Team management cringed at the criticism, but Tiger fans weren't finished throwing things at players to express their anger.

On Opening Day 1957, umpire Bill Summers was knocked down when a fan chucked a whiskey bottle at him, hitting him in the leg. "It would have killed me if it had hit me on the head," Summers lamented to the *Detroit News.*

The *News* quipped: "The empty bottle that struck Umpire Bill Summers originally contained Canadian whisky. In the search for the scoundrel who threw it, Tiger sleuths can exonerate Scotch and bourbon drinkers."

The scoundrel was never found, but Tiger general manager Spike Briggs vowed to tighten security to stem the rowdiness in the stands.

If Briggs followed through on his promise, it didn't work. On Opening Day against the Chicago White Sox two years later, Tiger fans staged what *Detroit Free Press* columnist George Puscas called "the biggest knockdown, drag-out fight the town has seen at a sporting event. The bleachers erupted so that you'd swear they had a battery of mortar guns up there. Guys were seen flying through the air, hurled or knocked from the upper rows of seats, and Johnny Callison, the White Sox center fielder, had his head opened by a brick."

In 1961, when Roger Maris was on his way to breaking Babe Ruth's single-season home-run record, Tiger fans infamously threw seat cushions at him. (The movie *61** embellished the incident, showing a fan throwing an actual seat at the Yankee right fielder.) That same season, Tiger Stadium bleacherites hurled a foot-long hammer at a favorite target, Cleveland Indians outfielder Jimmy Piersall, who said the lone projectile showed that Tiger fans were getting better, since they usually chucked multiple items at him.

"There have been fewer things thrown in this series than any I've played in a long time," the irrepressible Piersall told the Associated Press. "I just hope this improvement continues."

After the Tigers lost Game Seven of the 1934 World Series, bitter fans expressed outrage by ripping home plate out of the Navin Field turf.

98

During a game in 1968, Tiger fans pelted Red Sox right-fielder Ken "Hawk" Harrelson with cherry bombs. The public-address announcer pleaded in vain for the fans to stop. Harrelson refused to go back to his position for the ninth inning, choosing to stand behind second base instead.

"I wasn't about to go out there again," Harrelson told the *Detroit News* after the game. "[The fans] behaved like animals. One of those cherry bombs they threw landed less than 15 feet away from me. A little closer and, who knows, I may have been blinded for life."

The contentious 1972 American League Championship Series between the Tigers and Oakland A's went the full five games, with the A's edging the host Tigers, 2–1, in the final contest. During and after the game, Tiger fans again showed their ugly side.

"About those fans," the *Detroit News'* columnist Doug Bradford wrote. "A few of them descended onto the playing field before the last out, and time had to be called. They tossed rolls of paper, beer cans and the like onto the outfield grass in their usual display of lousy sportsmanship on the lousy day the Tigers lost the pennant."

The 1979 home opener was twice delayed because of inclement weather before the Tigers finally played the Texas Rangers on April 7. The Opening Day crowd was not in a good mood, as the Tigers booted the ball on their way to an 8–2 loss. Center fielder Ron LeFlore, who went 0 for 4 and made two errors that let in three runs, drew most of the fans' ire, as they booed him and threw bottles at him.

"If I have a great year, they'll all want to cheer me," LeFlore told the *Detroit Free Press*. "Let them get it off their chests now."

But tossing bottles at their hometown center fielder didn't exorcise the fans' demons, and the long-standing rowdiness and lawbreaking in the bleachers finally came to a head during the 1980 season.

The *Free Press*'s 1980 Opening Day special section featured a "consumer's guide to Tiger Stadium" that illustrated how lax things had gotten in the bleachers and the blasé attitude toward drug use.

Under the heading "Marijuana," the *Freep* warned:

> *It is illegal in Michigan and it is smoked all over the place in Tiger Stadium, especially in the bleachers, especially on Friday nights. If you insist on lighting up, please keep in mind that a lot of people object to smoke of any kind blowing in their faces, and that others object to people breaking the law in front of them. Once in a while, somebody will get arrested for it, so keep it down and don't complain if you get busted because you have been warned.*

If anyone heeded the warning, it didn't show.

The bleachers had been renovated in the 1979–80 off-season as part of the stadium overhaul that began in 1977. The ancient green wood benches gave way to blue aluminum bleachers that seated 10,500 fans. A city surcharge had been added to tickets to pay for the renovation, driving the price of a bleacher ticket up to two dollars. Despite the new trappings, old habits remained firmly in place.

On May 20, 1980, thirteen people were arrested and several others injured during a game against the Yankees. Throughout the entire game, fans brawled with police, security guards and each other; peppered cops with beer cups; set off firecrackers; and hurled bottles and a smoke bomb onto the field.

"Our town suffered another black eye last night," *Detroit News* columnist Joe Falls wrote.

> *At the worst possible time, too—with all of those New York writers in town. They saw another shameful display by our baseball fans, who brawled in the bleachers almost from start to finish during the long game against the Yankees. The bodies were flying everywhere. So were the fists. The cops were battling to keep peace. They wrestled with the fans and threw them down the stairs. It was like open warfare out there. It's scary.*

Team management beefed up security. It didn't help.

"I recently attended a Detroit Tigers vs. the Angels baseball game," wrote Mario D'Andrea of Farmington Hills, Michigan, in the June 10, 1980 letters-to-the-editor section of the *Detroit News*. Despite the Tiger victory, he wrote, "I regretted having attended the game. Seated directly in front of me were six gentlemen, more like pigs, whose only reason for being at this game was to test their tolerance for beer and my tolerance for them. I can put up with most rowdy behavior. But when one of these 'gentlemen' thought it humorous to drop his pants and expose his behind, that was too much."

On June 16, during a doubleheader against the Milwaukee Brewers, Tiger Stadium bleacherites were in rare form, fighting and littering the field with debris throughout both games. They threw firecrackers at Brewer outfielders Gorman Thomas and Sixto Lezcano. Six people were arrested for disorderly conduct, fourteen others ticketed and another fifteen ejected from the ballpark.

"They're good fans here, and I hate to knock 'em…but the people in the centerfield bleachers have been, by far, the rowdiest group I've ever seen," the *Free Press* quoted Tiger first baseman Richie Hebner—who had played two seasons in Philadelphia, where fans are notoriously rowdy.

General manager Jim Campbell had seen enough. The day after the raucous doubleheader, he ordered the bleachers closed until further notice. "I'm just goddamn fed up with them," Campbell told the *Free Press*, discussing the bleacherites. "I'm sick and tired. It's dangerous. It gives the city a bad name."

The bleachers were closed for two weeks before reopening on June 30 under new rules. Beer sales were restricted. The size of beer cups was reduced. Beach-ball bouncing, which had sparked many fights, was banned.

The closing of the Tiger Stadium bleachers was a national story; another embarrassment for Detroit.

The worst was yet to come.

DESPITE THE LONG, RICH history of the Detroit Tigers and the fantastic players who have donned the Olde English *D* through the years, as of 2019, the team had won only four World Championships. Three of the four celebrations are recalled fondly.

After the Tigers won their first title by beating the Chicago Cubs in the 1935 World Series, Detroiters danced in the streets, cheered, honked automobile horns and tossed confetti from the tall buildings downtown. While there were a few arrests, mostly for disturbing the police and public drunkenness, the celebration is regarded by many as one of the most joyful in Detroit history. After the 1945 Series win, Detroiters were still in feel-good mode from the U.S. victory over Japan in World War II only two months earlier, and the postgame festivities were without major incident.

When the Tigers improbably came back from a 3–1 deficit in the 1968 World Series to beat the powerful St. Louis Cardinals, it set off a raucous Detroit party that's discussed to this day, although the celebration was marred by a few serious incidents. Two men were fatally shot. Three men raped a seventeen-year-old girl in a downtown Detroit park; her screams couldn't be heard above the honking horns and cheers. An eight-year-old boy was shot in the foot, and someone struck a sixty-year-old man in the head, causing a severe laceration.

Despite the problems, the 1968 season, culminating in the victory celebration, is often cited by historians as an important step in the city's recovery from the worst riot in U.S. history, which had raged less than a year earlier.

The celebration after the Tigers came from behind to win the 1968 World Series is remembered fondly, although there were some problems during the festivities, including two men being fatally shot and a woman being raped downtown.

Then, there's 1984. When folks talk about that World Series celebration, they usually aren't smiling.

It was a rollicking season from the start. The talented Tigers won their first nine games and continued to a thirty-five and five record, the best forty-game start in baseball history.

The Tigers clinched the American League Eastern Division title at home against the Milwaukee Brewers. They also copped the pennant at home, easily dispatching the Royals in the ALCS, never trailing during the three-game sweep.

On October 14, 1984, a gray, drizzly Sunday, the Tigers were poised for another home celebration—the big one. The Tigers were up three games to one against the San Diego Padres in the World Series. There was an anxious buzz as Tiger fans began gathering around the ballpark hours before the game's scheduled 4:45 p.m. start. Thousands of diehards didn't have tickets to the game but wanted to be part of the celebration if the Tigers clinched the championship. The many bars that surrounded Tiger Stadium were packed with standing-room-only crowds, while dozens of people milled outside the bars—many of whom openly slammed beers and shots, in flagrant violation of the law. The cops let it slide.

There were thousands of Detroit police officers in the area in squad cars, on foot, on motorcycles and on horseback. During the late innings, most of the boots on the ground walked into the stadium, although several continued patrolling the streets. Detroit police were augmented by Wayne County sheriffs and cops from other local and federal departments.

When Tiger left fielder Larry Herndon caught Tony Gwinn's fly ball at 7:41 p.m., sealing the Tigers' fourth world championship, thousands of fans swarmed the field, rendering the battalion of cops lining the fences impotent. As Detroit right fielder Kirk Gibson weaved through the crowd toward the Tiger dugout, NBC's camera focused on a fan slowly arcing his fist toward Gibson's face, as if he were pretending to punch him. Gibby shoved the man aside and stalked into the dugout.

It was downhill from there.

Thousands of people who hadn't attended the game stormed the Tiger Stadium gates and rushed the field, tearing up strips of sod. Outside the ballpark, the celebration started innocently enough. Mounted police and officers on foot patrol hopped from one gathering to another, trying to quell smaller problems before they escalated.

But things quickly got ugly. A man climbed onto the roof of a bus, shed his clothes and danced naked. The crowd laughed and applauded—until someone coldcocked him with a whiskey bottle. The unfortunate reveler doubled over, holding his jaw and wailing in pain while dozens of drunken onlookers jeered.

That incident seemed to kindle the crowd's dark side. A clique of men started rocking Checker Cab no. 1267 before finally overturning it. Next, they zeroed in on a police car, smashing the overhead lights and ripping wires out of the engine before flipping the vehicle over and setting it on fire. As the black smoke billowed into the night sky, a rumor surfaced that Tiger Stadium was burning.

Cops swung their billy clubs at the rowdier members of the crowd as the officers were pelted with bottles, bricks and other debris. Some peaceful

A Detroit police officer in riot gear surveys the damage done by unruly fans following the Tigers' 1984 World Series win. It was one of the most notorious sports riots in U.S. history.

celebrants said they also were clubbed by overly aggressive, baton-wielding cops. Among them was *Detroit Free Press* religion writer Ruth Seymour.

Members of the national media stood on the Tiger Stadium ramp overlooking Michigan Avenue, watching the madness unfold on the street below—and taking notes.

A seventeen-year-old resident of suburban Lincoln Park, Kenneth "Bubba" Helms, became the symbol of the riot after an Associated Press photographer snapped his picture as he posed in front of a burning police car hoisting a Tiger pennant, his potbelly peeking out from under his shirt.

Helms said he'd guzzled Jim Beam bourbon and smoked marijuana while watching the game with his buddies before they decided to head downtown to join the celebration. When he saw photographers snapping pictures of an overturned, burning police car near the intersection of Michigan and Trumbull, Helms said he ran in front of the car and posed. "I just ran right over there," he told the *Free Press*.

"I gotta go get my picture taken," Helms claims he told his buddy. He said he saw a battery of photographers and "just jumped right in front of them and stood as still as I could," he said. The photographers snapped away.

"I was too drunk," he said. "I was just having a good time. It was the best time of my life. Serious."

At about 11:00 p.m., the hours-long drizzle turned into a sudden, heavy downpour. Police said that prevented further harm, as thousands of drunken, sopping-wet fans staggered homeward.

Mother Nature helped, but the damage was done. By the time the smoke cleared, four police cars, a motorcycle and a taxicab were torched; two vans from the local ABC affiliate, WXYZ (Channel 7), were overturned.

While the upside-down cars and fires shocked the national media—in large part because reporters stood on the Tiger Stadium ramp, watching it from just a few yards away—more serious crimes occurred outside their view.

An Ann Arbor man was fatally shot near the popular Lafayette Coney Island restaurant after robbers unsuccessfully tried to steal his wallet containing sixty-seven dollars. Three women reported being raped; two of the victims told police a man forced himself into their car, which was crawling through the downtown crowd, ordered them to drive a few blocks away to a more secluded area and then sexually assaulted and robbed them. Several purse-snatchings and muggings were reported.

Police made forty-two arrests, while Detroit Receiving Hospital staff said they treated several people who'd been cut, bruised, punched or stepped on during the riot.

When the heavy rains hit, Helms said he and his buddies headed back to Lincoln Park. Somewhere along the way, he said he got into a fistfight with someone over ownership of a strip of Tiger Stadium sod. The group stopped at a party store and bought a case of Budweiser before they dropped off Helms near his house. He said he never made it home but passed out "face down in the mud" on a neighbor's front lawn.

Earlier in the day, before he headed downtown, Helms had told his sister he hoped to get media coverage. He got his wish. The Associated Press picture of Helms appeared in newspapers across the country, including the *New York Post*, which ran the photo under the headline "World Series Rampage."

The *New York Daily News*' headline screamed, "Victory's Ugly Fire," with columnist Mike Lupica predicting: "This will not go away, this sight Sunday night of dead cabs and dead police cars 50 yards from Tiger Stadium... if you were there on Sunday night, you won't remember Gibson's home runs, or the cheers of the crowd. You will remember sirens, and smoke, and Checker Cab #1267 on fire and upside down. You will remember what a phrase—fan violence—looks like exactly. It is something for everyone to think about."

Detroit police chief William Hart, who would later go to prison for embezzlement, came under fire because he hadn't rescheduled a promotional examination that Sunday, meaning hundreds of officers who could have been deployed to Tiger Stadium were instead taking the test. Critics said Hart should have known there was a chance the Tigers could clinch the championship that night.

In addition to being a national embarrassment, the fans' behavior stoked long-simmering racial animosity and hostilities between city dwellers and suburbanites.

When Detroit city councilman Mel Ravitz complained that the national media was referring to the incident as a riot, fellow councilman Clyde Cleveland told the *Free Press*: "Riots are for black folks. When it's white folks from the suburbs, it's a victory celebration."

Redford Township resident Nicholas LaBate, twenty, was charged with arson in connection with the torching of the police car. Two Detroit Police reserves testified they saw LaBate near the squad car with something burning in his hand.

During LaBate's arraignment, Thirty-Sixth District Court magistrate Willie Lipscomb ripped into the defendant. "Many working people in this city couldn't even get a ticket for the games," he said, according to the *Detroit News*. "They were sold out and populated in the main by suburbanites who day in and day out criticize this city and then come down and burn it up, and give us who live here a bad name."

LaBate was later found not guilty. He filed a lawsuit against the city and the reserve police officers, claiming the cops had assaulted him and that he was arrested without probable cause. The lawsuit was thrown out.

Detroit mayor Coleman Young tried to tamp down the rhetoric, calling on people to stop blaming suburbanites for the rowdiness. "I think it is unfortunate a few jerks caused some problems," he told United Press International. "I don't think it is important whether they came from Detroit or outside Detroit. I don't think we need to use the occasion of a great victory to start a fight between Detroit and its suburbs."

The mayor also lamented the way the national media were characterizing the incident. "Everyone knows there was no riot," Young said. "We had some overexuberant and over-drunken fans who got carried away."

Despite the mayor's protests, local and national reporters continue to use the "R" word when referring to what happened outside Tiger Stadium following the Tigers' 8–4 win over the Padres.

There was a sad postscript for Helms, the 1984 World Series riot's poster boy. Immediately after the Series, he enjoyed a short period of notoriety; Halloween was only two weeks after the incident, and many people in the Detroit area dressed as Bubba Helms. But things quickly went sour. The longtime weed smoker and drinker got hooked on hard drugs and moved to Tennessee to start a new life. Bad times and addiction followed him, and in April 2001, he put a shotgun in his mouth and pulled the trigger, killing himself.

In the end, Lupica's prediction didn't come true—the destruction that followed the 1984 World Series hasn't overshadowed Gibson's homer, which is etched as one of the most iconic moments in Tiger history.

Unfortunately, though, so is the image of the pudgy, stoned suburbanite, who, like Gibson, had an unforgettable photo snapped of him with his arms raised in celebration.

8

BILLY THE BATTLER

No discussion about the Detroit Tigers and mayhem would be complete without a dive into the complicated, paranoid psyche of one Alfred Manuel Pesano Jr.

People called him Billy, and later, Billy Martin—and a whole lot of other not-so-nice names. Usually, he asked for it.

Martin is unquestionably the most combative manager in Tiger history. He probably was the most combative manager in the histories of the New York Yankees, Texas Rangers, Oakland A's and Minnesota Twins as well.

"I'm afraid I'd never make a good ambassador—I'd start a war or two," Martin told the *Detroit News*. It may have been an understatement.

Some modern baseball fans lament the introduction of replay into the game, because it has all but eliminated arguments between managers and umpires. But if Martin were managing today, he'd probably argue with the umps anyway, no matter what the video showed.

When it came to running a ball club, Martin was a genius, and he's usually listed among the greatest managers of all time. But he always wore out his welcome.

Martin is best remembered nationally for his time in New York. His drunken skirmishes and feuds with Yankee owner George Steinbrenner made the Berkeley, California native a household name. His 1977 dugout blowup with right fielder Reggie Jackson was legendary.

But Martin was no slouch in Detroit, getting mixed up in one of the most epic brawls in the city's violent history while he was a visiting manager and, a few years later, winning an unlikely division title as the Tiger skipper.

Volatile Tiger manager Billy Martin squares off against an Oakland Athletics player after a brawl at Tiger Stadium on August 22, 1972.

He was born on May 16, 1928, to parents Alfred and Joan Pesano. Alfred Senior abandoned the family when Junior was eight months old. Soon after that, Joan changed the family surname to Martin. The baby's maternal grandmother called him Belli or Bellitz, which was shortened to Billy.

Martin wasn't big, but he was a cyclone on the Berkeley ball diamonds. After graduating from high school in 1946, he was offered a contract by the Idaho Falls Russets in the Pioneer League. He bounced around a few minor-league clubs, playing for Oakland Oaks manager Casey Stengel, who left to manage the Yankees.

Martin was reunited with Stengel in October 1949, when he was sold to the Yankees. He made his major-league debut on April 18, 1950, and got 2 hits in the eighth inning of a 15–10 Yankee win over the Boston Red Sox.

Despite the auspicious start, Martin was sent to the minors, although he was called back up about a month later when the Yankees traded their regular second baseman, Snuffy Stirnweiss, to the St. Louis Browns. Martin hit a pedestrian .250 in his first full season, although he quickly established a reputation as a clutch hitter with a solid glove.

That off-season, Martin and Yankee teammates Whitey Ford and Bob Brown were drafted into the military. Martin joined the army, serving for five months during the 1950–51 off-season until he was granted a hardship exemption because he was financially responsible for his wife, mother, sister and stepfather.

The Yankees were allowed to keep the drafted players on their roster, enabling Martin to appear as a pinch-runner in the 1951 World Series, although he didn't get an at bat. The Yankees beat the crosstown New York Giants in six games, and Martin copped his first of four world championship rings as a player.

Martin missed the first few weeks of the 1952 season after he broke his right ankle while showing how he slid into bases during a television show hosted by Yankee legend Joe DiMaggio, who had retired after the previous season.

When Martin returned to the roster, he had the first of many high-profile fights in his career, tangling with Red Sox rookie shortstop Jimmy Piersall under the Fenway Park stands. Weeks later, there was another Martin scuffle, this time with Browns catcher Clint Courtney.

Because of his penchant for fighting, newspaper reporters began referring to the scrappy second baseman as "One-round Billy Martin."

Martin distinguished himself in the 1952 World Series, a tightly contested seven-game affair against the Brooklyn Dodgers. The highlight came in the seventh inning of Game Seven, when Martin made a great running catch of a popup by fellow second baseman Jackie Robinson in a crucial situation: two outs and the bases loaded, with the Yankees holding on to a 4–2 lead. The wind played tricks with the popup, and Yankee infielders, apparently confused, stumbled around until Martin dashed across the grass and made a shoestring catch.

The next year, Martin got into another fight with Courtney and scrapped with Tiger catcher Matt Batts. After the fight with Batts, Martin lamented to the Associated Press his growing status as "the bad boy of baseball." "They gave me a reputation as a fighter, and now every guy and his brother is trying to make me earn it," Martin told the Associated Press.

Sure, I had some fights in the field, but I never started any of them. The other day in Detroit, Matt Batts tagged me at the plate and then banged me on the nose while I was lying on the ground. What was I supposed to do? Say "thank-you?" Every city we go into fans holler at me, "hey, Martin, who are going to start a fight with today?"…I can't understand it. I always thought that people admired you for sticking up for your rights.

Martin's manager, Stengel, supported the player. "Billy's being hit with the hardest blocks this side of a professional football field," he told UPI.

The battling second baseman was one of the heroes of the 1953 World Series, driving in the run that netted the Yankees their fifth consecutive world championship with a base hit in the bottom of the ninth inning against Dodger pitcher Clem Labine. Martin broke an all-time record for a six-game series with 23 total bases, 4 more than the previous record-holder, Babe Ruth, had racked up in the 1923 Fall Classic. Martin ended up with a .500 batting average with 5 extra-base hits and 2 triples, tying the record for a six-game World Series. His play earned him the Babe Ruth Memorial Award, which was a precursor to the World Series Most Valuable Player award.

After facing Martin in the series, Brooklyn pitcher Carl Erskine told reporters: "It's hard to believe but players like [Yankee shortstop] Phil Rizzuto and Billy Martin give me a lot more trouble than hitters like Mickey Mantle and Yogi Berra. You just can't strike out Rizzuto and Martin. At least I can't anyway."

Martin was reclassified by the Berkeley, California draft board as 1-A in January 1954 and was drafted into the army. He appealed the decision, claiming again that he was solely responsible for taking care of his family, including his wife, Lois, from whom he had separated after their marriage in 1950. His appeal was denied.

Always complaining people were out to get him, Martin applied for a hardship discharge from the army, claiming he was being treated unfairly by his superior officers at Fort Ord, California, where he was going through basic training. Martin said he wasn't being given as many weekend passes as his fellow recruits and that he was barred from playing on the base's ball club. His appeal for a hardship discharge was denied.

After basic training, Martin was deployed to Fort Carson, Colorado, where he served in the Sixty-First Infantry Regiment and managed the base's ball club to a 15-2 record.

Martin missed most of the 1954 and 1955 seasons, although the army granted him an extended furlough in 1955, allowing him to play in the World Series against the Dodgers. During the Series, Martin further established his reputation as a brawler when he tried to steal home in Game One. After he was tagged out, he got into a shoving match with the usually friendly Brooklyn catcher Roy Campanella.

"I wasn't sore," Martin told the AP. "I just don't like being pushed around. I might have punched him in the nose if it hadn't been the World

Series." Martin's fighting words notwithstanding, there were no further incidents in the Series.

After losing to the Yankees in the 1947, 1949, 1952 and 1953 World Series, Brooklyn finally won its first world championship in 1955 by beating the Bronx Bombers in seven games. Despite the loss, Martin again had a fine Series, hitting .320 with 8 hits and 4 RBIs. Although Martin had played only twenty games during the 1955 season, his teammates voted to give him the full $5,598 share of the losing teams' World Series bonus.

On-field success didn't diminish Martin's rage. In May 1957, he got into another scrap, and this highly publicized fight caused him to be traded.

Martin and his drinking buddy, Mickey Mantle, had celebrated Martin's birthday at New York City's hottest nightclub, the Copacabana. Other Yankees, including Yogi Berra, Hank Bauer and Whitey Ford, and their wives eventually joined the party.

A bowling team was sitting at a nearby table, and one of the intoxicated members reportedly began hurling racial slurs at entertainer Sammy Davis Jr., who was performing at the club. Bauer, an ex-marine, took exception. An argument escalated into a full-scale donnybrook, and Martin, as usual, was in the middle of it.

When the dust cleared, Yankee management traded Martin to the Kansas City Athletics. For years afterward, Martin would complain that he was made the scapegoat for the drunken capers of his more-talented buddies, Hall-of-Famers Mantle and Ford.

Martin finished the 1957 season in Kansas City, playing seventy-three games and hitting .257. About a month after the season ended, Martin and five other players were traded to the Tigers. Martin wasn't happy with the trade, demanding a cash settlement from the A's and threatening to hold out until he got paid.

"They just can't throw us (players) around from one club to another without us having a say-so," Martin complained to an Associated Press reporter immediately after the trade. "I don't have any argument with Detroit. My argument is with the Kansas City Athletics. If I am a tool of this great machine of baseball, I want to get something out of it."

Martin never was compensated for the A's trade, and he played the 1958 season in Detroit without any reported fights, although his stint on the Tigers was far from uneventful. Since Frank Bolling was the Tigers' established second baseman, Martin was slated to play shortstop. But he lost his starting position to Coot Veal, and Martin became a part-time fill-in at third base. According to the *Detroit Free Press*, Martin's Tiger teammates resented his bombast.

"After Martin had prowled the dugout steps as was his habit, hollering jibes at a rival during infield practice, a Tiger teammate said: 'All right, you can quiet down now. Everyone knows pepperpot Billy Martin is around,'" the paper reported.

After the season, on November 21—a year and a day after his trade to Detroit—the Tigers swapped him and relief pitcher Al Cicotte to Cleveland for pitchers Don Mossi and Ray Narleski. After the trade, Martin complained to a *Free Press* reporter: "I can't understand it. These fellows [his Tiger teammates] didn't seem to want to win." The *Free Press* concluded, "Martin felt he was being blamed for the Tigers' failures to be a factor in the American League race."

Martin spent an uneventful 1959 season in Cleveland before the Indians traded him to the Cincinnati Reds in December—the fourth time he was traded in less than three years. During the 1960 season, Martin got into another fight, this time with Chicago Cubs pitcher Jim Brewer. On August 6, in the second inning of a game in Chicago's Wrigley Field, Brewer threw a high and tight pitch that ricocheted off Martin's bat and hit him in the head. When Martin swung and missed at the next pitch, he let go of his bat during the follow-through, sending the club flying toward the pitcher's mound. Martin walked toward the mound to retrieve his bat, but Brewer picked it up first. Martin pretended to reach for the bat but instead sucker-punched the Cubs pitcher, fracturing the orbital bone near his right eye. A bench-clearing brawl followed, after which Martin was ejected from the game.

While Martin got a trip to the showers, Brewer got a trip to the hospital, where he was treated for his fracture. His injury finished him for the season.

National League president Warren Giles suspended Martin for five days and fined him $500. Once again, Martin said he was being made the scapegoat.

"Brewer threw at my head and nobody is going to do that," Martin complained to the AP. "I was in the hospital last year when I got hit in the face and had seven fractures. Nobody is going to throw at my head again. That first pitch by Brewer was behind my head and Cub pitchers knocked me down three times on Wednesday."

Because they'd lost their pitcher for the season, the Cubs sued Martin for $1 million in damages. The case was litigated for nine years before Martin finally settled for $10,000.

The Reds, like the Yankees, A's and Tigers before them, quickly tired of Martin's act, selling him to the Milwaukee Braves. Martin played only six games for the Braves in 1961; the former Tiger Bolling once again barred him from a starting second-base job.

In June, the Braves traded Martin to the Minnesota Twins for shortstop (and later Tiger coach) Billy Consolo. Martin played 108 games for the Twins, hitting .246, eleven points below his lifetime batting average. During spring training in 1962, Martin retired as a player.

The Twins hired Martin as a special scout, and he served in that capacity until 1965, when Minnesota management named him the team's third-base coach. Three years later, in June 1968, Martin was hired as manager of the Twins' AAA farm club, the Denver Bears of the Pacific Coast League.

In October 1968, Martin was named the Twins' manager, succeeding Cal Ermer. The team had decided to hire Martin when the season ended but held off announcing the move until after the Fall Classic.

Thus began one of the greatest—and most bellicose—managerial careers in baseball history.

Martin's talent in the dugout was on full display his first year as a big-league manager. He took a team that had finished in seventh place the year before with a drab 79-83 record and won the American League West title with a 97-65 mark. (The 1969 season was the first in which the leagues were bifurcated into divisions.)

But if the 1969 season gave the world a glimpse of how great a manager Martin was, it also revealed, for those not already aware, his dark side. When the Twins visited Detroit on August 6, Martin severely beat one of his pitchers, sending him to the hospital.

The incident, one of the most infamous of Martin's career, happened in an alley behind the popular Lindell AC bar in downtown Detroit. According to longtime *Detroit News* sports columnist Doc Greene, tempers flared after Boswell bad-mouthed one of Martin's longtime friends, Twins coach Art Fowler, who had told Martin the pitcher hadn't completed the required number of pregame laps.

"That's enough of that," Greene quoted Martin as saying to his pitcher. "Go home and go to bed now. You're all through for the night. I'll be up to your room later to talk about it."

Greene said Boswell and his roommate, Twins outfielder Bob Allison, walked out of the bar's rear exit and into the alley behind Cass Avenue. When Allison tried to explain to Boswell that Fowler was the manager's close friend, Boswell sucker-punched him, according to Greene, who said bar owner Jimmy Butsicaris and others tried to break up the fight.

"About that time, Martin showed up," Greene wrote. "'You're a big, brave one, aren't you?' said Billy."

Boswell reportedly replied, "I'll take a piece of you, you little Dago squirt," before throwing a punch at Martin.

"Martin began riveting away at Boswell's stomach, changing his attack every two or three punches to Boswell's head," Greene recounted. "He was wearing his Yankee World Series ring. He punched Boswell across the alley and up against the brick wall that forms the fourth wall to the bar. He clipped him once more on the jaw as Boswell tried to fall away from the building. The police showed up. Jimmy [Butsicaris] waved them away. Jimmy took Boswell back in the bar, throwing all the other patrons out, and spent the next 20 minutes reviving Boswell. Then, he took him to Ford Hospital. There, Dave had his face stitched up."

Boswell required twenty stitches for his injuries. Martin later claimed he was merely coming to Allison's rescue. Boswell insisted of Martin, "He really mauled me…he isn't telling the truth if he says I went after him."

Twins owner Cal Griffith wasn't happy about his manager beating up one of his best pitchers, but the team kept winning, so Martin's job was safe—for the time being.

During the best-of-five American League Championship Series, the Twins were swept by the Baltimore Orioles, one of the greatest teams of all time. A few days after the loss, Martin experienced what would be a pattern for the rest of his time in baseball: Despite his wonderful record on the field, he was fired.

Martin was taking heat for some of the decisions he'd made during the ALCS against the Orioles. One move that was heavily panned was his Game Three decision to start Bob Miller, who was knocked out of the game in the second inning when the Orioles scored three runs.

When the team owner asked Martin why he'd started Miller, who had posted a mediocre 5-5 record during the regular season, according to the *Miami News*, Martin shot back, "Because I'm the manager, that's why."

Griffith fired him days later.

"Billy is popular to a certain degree," Griffith told a *Miami News* reporter after giving his skipper the pink slip. "You know Billy can go into a crowd and charm the hell out of you, but he ignored me. I asked him to come in and see me several times and he didn't. I think the Twins are just as much a part of me as they are of Billy Martin."

Martin was out of baseball for a year after being fired. He took a job at Minneapolis radio station KDWB, where he hosted a morning sports show. That summer, rumors that Martin was about to be hired to manage the Oakland A's were rampant. The scuttlebutt turned out to be false, but one wonders how Martin would have coexisted with the "Swingin' A's" of the early 1970s, an all-time great team that was infamous for its fractured clubhouse.

Instead of taking the A's job, in October 1970, Martin was named as the twenty-sixth manager of the Detroit Tigers. He succeeded Mayo Smith, who had guided the team to a world championship only three years earlier but posted a disappointing 79-83 mark in 1970, Detroit's worst record in seven years.

"(Martin's) job in Detroit is to shake up a team that became complacent and slipped downward," *Detroit News* sportswriter Watson Spoelstra observed.

Martin was an immediate success. In 1971, the Tigers posted a 91-71 record, second behind the powerhouse Orioles and their four twenty-game winners.

As with any Martin team, there were bumps in the road. In August, Martin almost came to blows with Red Sox outfielder Reggie Smith after a bench-clearing brawl during a 12–11 Boston win. Following the game, as Smith walked to his car in the Fenway Park parking lot, Martin reportedly yelled at him: "Hey, you've got a big mouth from 90 feet away. You looking for a fight?" According to multiple newspaper accounts, Smith replied that he was game, and the two men squared off until Fowler, now a Tiger coach (who followed Martin to other teams throughout his career), intervened.

A month later, as the season wound down, Martin pulled popular outfielder Willie Horton off the field because the skipper claimed the outfielder failed to hustle down the baseline on a groundout. Horton had been in Martin's doghouse all season; the rift was so bad, Horton refused to pose for the team photo.

Things got infinitely better the following season, when Martin guided the Tigers to their first AL Eastern Division title. Detroit's 86-70 record was a half game better than the Boston Red Sox, setting up a showdown with the Western Division champion A's.

The heroes of 1968 took the talented Athletics to the wire, losing in five games. The most memorable incident happened in the bottom of the seventh inning of Game Two in Oakland.

Tiger relief pitcher Lerrin LaGrow threw a fastball that nipped A's shortstop Bert "Campy" Campaneris in the left ankle. Campaneris hurled his bat at LaGrow, who ducked a split-second before the Louisville Slugger helicoptered inches from his head.

Not surprisingly, Martin seemed to be angrier than LaGrow.

"Well, excitement aplenty," Tiger announcer George Kell drawled, describing the on-field action: "That's the umpires holding Billy Martin; he's trying to get at Campaneris."

It took the entire umpiring crew to hold Martin back. Eventually, Campaneris and LaGrow were ejected from the game, peace was restored and the A's went on to beat the Tigers, 3–2 to take a commanding two-games-to-none series lead.

After the game, Martin ripped into Campaneris. "I don't know what that idiot was thinking," he told the Associated Press. "He may have to talk to his psychiatrist to find out. You can bet your ass I was going out there for him. I'm not going to get after him now, but if there's ever another fight out there, I'm going out there and find him and beat the shit out of him."

The next day, American League president Joe Cronin suspended Campaneris for the rest of the ALCS, fined him $500 and suspended him for the first seven games of the 1973 regular season.

The Tigers lost the final game, 2–1, in Tiger Stadium. Emulating their team's manager, Tiger fans threw a fit, running on to the field, burning things and tossing rolls of toilet paper from the stands.

Martin was embroiled in yet another controversy during spring training in 1973. On March 27, Martin and rookie Ike Blessitt were arrested—although this time, Martin was playing peacemaker for a change. Witnesses said Blessitt was in a restaurant arguing with an attorney. Martin, who was sitting at a nearby table with Fowler, heard the dispute and took Blessitt outside to calm him down. Earlier that day, Martin had told the youngster he was sending him down to the minor leagues for more seasoning.

As the two men talked, a police cruiser rolled up. One of the officers got out and walked toward Martin and the player. "He came over to where we were and he said to Ike, 'Okay, black boy, you're arrested,'" Martin recounted to United Press International. "I said, 'he didn't do anything wrong,'" and the cop said, 'you're arrested, too.'"

The officer hauled both men to jail, and they were charged with using profanity in a public place. Martin paid their fines of thirty-two dollars each.

Three days later, Martin got himself into another flap. He had fined Horton for leaving early during a preseason game against the Red Sox, and general manager Jim Campbell held a meeting with the player and manager to discuss the infraction. During the meeting, Campbell said Martin told him, "find yourself another manager" before storming from the room. Campbell and Martin met the next day, and the manager didn't quit.

He wouldn't finish the season, though. On September 2, the Tigers fired him after he had served a three-day suspension for ordering his pitches to throw spitballs. Martin was angry that Cleveland pitcher Gaylord Perry was getting away with throwing spitballs, so Martin ordered his pitchers to also throw the illegal pitch and then admitted to reporters that he'd told his players to break the rules. League president Cronin slapped him with the three-day suspension.

Martin offered his opinion to the AP as to why Campbell fired him: "I think I just got too much publicity and he didn't like that. What happened is typical. I'm a perfectionist. I want to win. And along the way, I step on some toes; I do things that annoy people."

The Texas Rangers quickly hired Martin to replace Whitey Herzog as manager. Martin took a team that had lost one hundred games the previous season and led them to eighty-four wins and a second-place finish in 1974, his first full year as Rangers manager. The next year, with the team struggling and under new ownership, Martin was fired a few days after the All-Star break.

A week later, Yankee owner George Steinbrenner scooped up Martin to replace manager Bill Virdon, and a legendary, dysfunctional relationship was born. Martin and Steinbrenner feuded publicly, while Martin feuded with his players, most notably Reggie Jackson. The two almost came to blows in the visitors' dugout during a nationally televised game at Fenway Park in 1977.

Martin, not surprisingly, was a managerial success, guiding the Yankees to two straight World Series berths and a world championship his first two years with the team. Also, not surprisingly, he was fired during the 1978 season after saying of Steinbrenner and Jackson, "One's a born liar and the other convicted."

But Steinbrenner broke the pattern in 1979 by rehiring Martin—then, the Yankee owner fired his skipper at the end of the season.

Martin then was hired by the Oakland A's. His team played an aggressive style of baseball that came to be known as "Billyball." By 1981, the A's were back in the playoffs, losing to the Yankees in the ALCS. But after the A's faltered in 1982, with Martin being heavily criticized for overworking his pitching staff, he was fired again.

Steinbrenner hired Martin for a third time to manage the 1983 season—and fired him a month after the season ended. The merry-go-round continued in 1985, when Steinbrenner hired Martin again, only to fire him, as usual, at season's end. In 1987, Martin was hired for his fifth stint as Yankee manager, but only sixty-eight games into the 1988 season, he was canned again.

On Christmas Day 1989, Martin was the passenger in his pickup truck, which was driven by his good friend Bill Reedy, owner of the popular Reedy's Saloon in Detroit, down the street from Tiger Stadium. The pair had been drinking in an upstate New York bar, and Reedy decided to drive Martin's truck, which skidded off an icy road and tumbled three hundred feet down an embankment and flipped over. Martin, sixty-one, was killed; Reedy was badly injured.

Martin's legacy is tainted by alcohol and fisticuffs, but he left his mark on the field, as well. In a 1987 poll of former major leaguers, Martin was voted the eight-greatest manager of all time.

9

MISCELLANEOUS MAYHEM

T hrough the years, the Tigers and their fans have featured straight arrows, bad boys, nice guys, goofballs and punks. Some lived on the edge, drinking hard, cussing up a storm and never apologizing. At the Corner or away from home, the Tigers and their followers have found themselves in the middle of some strange, volatile situations.

THE TIGERS WERE LOCKED in a tight match against the Washington Senators on the afternoon of September 15, 1934, and Fred Hacker couldn't eat.

Hacker, forty-seven, a foreman at the Rouge Steel plant in Dearborn, Michigan, lay on his couch in his home at 6333 Mead in Dearborn listening to the Tiger game on WWJ radio. The Tigers were fighting for a pennant, and Hacker's wife told reporters he was anxious about the game's outcome.

"He believed the game to be a crucial one and thought a victory would assure him of the thrill he had looked forward to for weeks—seeing the Tigers in a World Series game," the *Detroit Free Press* reported.

Hacker's wife, referred to in articles only as "Mrs. Hacker," said her husband "had decided to put off eating until after the game's finish when he returned home from work," the *Free Press* said.

The game was a back-and-forth, exhilarating affair. The score was 1–1 going into the ninth inning, but the Senators scored a run to take the lead. In the bottom of the ninth, Tiger first baseman Hank Greenberg, whose throwing error in the top of the inning had allowed the go-ahead run to score, tied the game with a home run to left field. The contest then moved into extra innings.

Washington retook the lead in the eleventh inning on another throwing error, this time by Tiger left fielder Goose Goslin. But, as Greenberg had done earlier in the game, Goslin redeemed himself by knocking in the tying run with a sacrifice fly.

In the bottom of the twelfth inning, Tiger player-manager Mickey Cochrane rapped a single to score Tiger right fielder Pete Fox with the tying run. Then, Tiger second baseman Charlie Gerhinger blasted a walk-off home run deep into the right-field bleachers.

Hacker, listening to WWJ announcer Ty Tyson broadcast the action, couldn't take the excitement. "As word of Charlie Gehringer's twelfth-inning home run came over the radio…[Hacker's] tense figure suddenly slumped," the *Free Press* reported. "Death followed a few minutes later."

A generation earlier, during another Tiger pennant race, fan Paul J. Kraft also died while cheering for the Tigers.

Kraft was a thirty-nine-year-old wealthy wholesale liquor dealer from Adrian, Michigan, and a former infielder who had played on various Michigan semipro teams in the 1890s. He was battling cancer but made the seventy-mile trip from Adrian to Detroit the morning of Friday, October 11, 1907, to see his beloved Tigers face the powerhouse Chicago Cubs for Game Four of what was then referred to as the "world's series." The liquor dealer stayed at Lume's Stag Hotel at Monroe and Farmer Streets.

While at the hotel, Kraft "was attacked by a severe hemorrhage of the lungs," the *Detroit News* reported. "He retired thinking that a night's rest would restore him."

Going into the game—the first World Series contest ever played in Detroit—the Tigers were down in the series, two games to none. (Game One had ended in a 3–3 tie.) The Tigers took a 1–0 lead in the fourth inning, followed by a rain delay. When play resumed, Cubs pitcher Orval Overall gave his team a 2–1 lead when he knocked in two runners who'd been put on base via a walk and an error. The Tigers would eventually lose, 6–1.

It was all too much for Kraft, who was "stricken suddenly by convulsions at the championship game at Bennett Park," the *News* reported.

A wire story that ran in newspapers across the country said, "Kraft's frantic yelling for his team brought on hemorrhaging of the lungs."

After Kraft collapsed at the game, he was rushed to St. Mary's Hospital in Detroit. He died in the hospital at about 2:00 p.m. the next day. "Kraft suffered six convulsions before the end came and his death was most pitiful," the *News* said.

WILLIAM DOUGLAS STREET IS likely the most fraudulent person to ever wear a Detroit Tiger uniform—and for a team that employed Denny McLain, that's saying something.

Street's deceitful career inspired an award-winning movie. He impersonated an NFL player, scrubbed up for surgery while posing as a doctor in a Chicago hospital, fraudulently practiced as an attorney in Detroit and passed himself off as a *Time* magazine correspondent. It all started in 1971, when Street, whose father was a Detroit bus driver, lied his way into a tryout with the Tigers during spring training.

Street had been phoning Detroit's director of the team's farm operations, Hoot Evers, pretending to be Houston Oilers wide receiver Jerry LeVias. He said he was tired of football and wanted to try out for the Tigers if the team would foot the cost of a $165 airplane ticket.

Evers took the bait and sent the money. Not satisfied, Street walked into a Detroit bar owned by Tiger pinch-hitting great Gates Brown and, still posing as LeVias, said he'd lost his luggage on the way to the tryout. Brown loaned him $300. The Gator never got his money back.

The Tigers issued a press release touting the tryout and prepared the red carpet.

"They were primed for me when I got down there, man," Street told the *Detroit News*. "I don't know what kind of treatment I was expecting, but they put me in a uniform—and I always dug uniforms, know what I mean?—and then they brought the press around, and there I was. And that was the first time I found out how easy it was to get people to believe whatever you said, as long as you said it right."

But, after a few questions from the media, the *News* reported, "things started to go wrong. Levias/Strreet began to lay it on a little thick, firing some shots at his former employers, the Oilers, then telling reporters he thought he could make the big club, 'with half a season or so in the minors.'"

Meanwhile, back in Houston, the real Jerry Levias began reading wire reports about the tryout and tried to contact Oiler management to sort it all out.

It was only a matter of time before the fraud would unravel. That happened the

During spring training in 1971, the Tigers outfitted William Douglas Street with a uniform after he claimed to be Houston Oilers wide receiver Jerry LeVias who was tired of football and wanted to give baseball a try.

minute Street stepped onto the ball diamond. "Something was very clearly wrong with his fundamentals," head Tiger scout Ed Katalinas, who had discovered Baltimore high school outfielder Al Kaline twenty years earlier, told the *News*.

Tiger base-running instructor Bernie deViveiros expected blinding speed from a solid NFL wide receiver. Instead, "he didn't even look like an athlete," he told the *News*.

Street said the negative assessment of his performance by Tiger officials and coaches was "sour grapes" over how he'd bamboozled them. As far as his performance, Street told the *News*, "I think I did okay."

Although the scam fizzled, it was the launching pad for Street's long criminal career.

Weeks after his aborted tryout with the Tigers, Street dropped off a letter at the Detroit home of Tiger outfielder Willie Horton. Horton's wife answered the door, and the con artist handed her the note, which said he would kill the entire family if Willie didn't pay him $20,000. She recognized Street from being around him in spring training, and after he left, she called police. He was arrested.

"That was some troubled times," Willie Horton told the *News*. "We had to get security for my kids to go to school. What he put us through, I never wanted to see him again."

Street received twenty years' probation for the threat, but it didn't stop him. In the next few years, he would go on to pose as a University of Michigan defensive back at a 1972 college football all-star game and as a *Time* magazine reporter.

He was in and out of prison, and in 1975, he absconded from parole and went to Chicago. He said he found an old white lab coat and used it to pose as a doctor at Illinois Masonic Hospital. Street claimed he was in the emergency room helping out and was pressed into service to perform an emergency appendectomy because the doctor was late. Street's cover held up for the time being, because the real doctor showed up. He fooled the staff for three months until someone ran his Social Security number and found it matched a paroled prisoner.

"After serving more prison time, Street became an unofficial student at the University of Michigan Law School in 1983," the *News* reported. "He showed up dressed in a naval officer's uniform and managed to pull off the ruse for two semesters.

"He was sent back to prison after failing a background check performed by a law firm that had offered him a job, after cashing a $600 check stolen from a classmate, and after trying to register at Yale School of Medicine with a fake ID," the *News* said.

In his most recent caper, in 2016, Street was sentenced to thirty-six months in prison for posing as William Stratton, a U.S. Defense Department contractor.

Street's long and winding career as a con artist spans Michigan, California, Florida and Illinois. He racked up twenty-five convictions.

A movie about Street's career, *Chameleon Street*, won the top award at the 1990 Sundance Film Festival.

THE STREAKING CRAZE CAME to Tiger Stadium on Opening Day 1974, when several fans took off their clothes and ran naked through the bleachers in the windy, thirty-eight-degree weather during the Tigers' 3–0 loss to the New York Yankees. None of the nudists were arrested. One man didn't actually run but sat naked in his seat.

"If we would have arrested them, we'd have had a riot on our hands," Ralph Snyder, director of stadium operations, told the Associated Press.

Losing pitcher Mickey Lolich quipped to the *Windsor Star* of the nude cavorters, "It's merely a second childhood without diapers."

ON OCTOBER 13, 1977, Detroit police emergency lines were flooded with reports from concerned radio listeners reporting that a disc jockey for Detroit rock radio station WWWW FM (W4) was on the air threatening to kill himself because he was despondent over the recent deaths of his friends. Officers rushed to W4's facility on Jefferson Avenue, only to find out the whole thing was a prank cooked up by "shock jock" Steve Dahl, who had promised his audience "a radio first—a live, on-the-air suicide." Police officials were not amused at the waste of manpower.

After Dahl's stint in Detroit, during which he also worked for rock station WABX, he moved to Chicago, where, on July 12, 1979, he pulled off his most infamous stunt: Disco Demolition Night.

Rock 'n' roll fans had heavily slammed disco music since the genre began permeating pop culture following the 1977 blockbuster movie *Saturday Night Fever* and its accompanying soundtrack album. Rock radio stations capitalized on the growing animosity; in Detroit, WRIF started the D.R.E.A.D. (Detroit Rockers Engaged in the Abolition of Disco) Club. In Chicago, Dahl regularly bashed disco on his radio show on WLUP 97.9 FM.

Dahl and Mike Veeck, the son of White Sox owner Bill Veeck, came up with a promotion: Anyone who brought a disco record to the Comiskey Park ticket gate would be charged only ninety-eight cents for a doubleheader against the Tigers. Dahl said he would blow up the collected records in a huge bin in the outfield between games.

Comiskey Park sold out, with thousands of people hanging around outside the gates. During the first game, which the Tigers won, 4–1, records that hadn't been collected at the gates were flung like Frisbees onto the field.

"They would slice around you and stick in the ground," Tiger designated hitter Rusty Staub told the *New York Times*. "It wasn't just one, it was many. Oh, God almighty, I've never seen anything so dangerous in my life. I begged the guys to put on their batting helmets."

Tiger outfielder Ron LeFlore said golf balls bearing the message "Disco sucks" also were thrown at him.

"Whiskey bottles were flying over our dugout," Tiger pitcher Jack Morris told the *Times*.

"I remember from the get-go, it wasn't a normal crowd," Tiger shortstop Alan Trammell told the *Times*. "The outfielders were definitely a little scared."

Mike Veeck said the team hired enough security guards to handle the expected 35,000 fans. Although the official attendance was announced as 47,795, thousands crashed the gates, and Veeck said there were close to 60,000 people in the jam-packed stands.

"People brought ladders," Staub told the *Times*. "They were climbing in from the outside. It was like a riot."

After Tiger relief pitcher Aurelio Lopez struck out White Sox third baseman Jim Morrison to end the first game, Dahl, clad in a military-style jacket decorated with buttons bearing anti-disco slogans, marched onto the field, thanked the fans and led them in a chant of "Disco sucks."

Dahl then donned a camouflage army helmet and made his way to the crate in center field containing the thousands of records that had been collected.

"We rock-&-rollers will resist, and we will triumph," he screamed into the microphone. He then counted to three. After a several-second delay, a series of explosions rocked Comiskey Park, and smoke billowed as debris from the destroyed records rained down on the outfield grass.

Fans cheered, but the riot hadn't yet started. First, Dahl sang an off-key rendition of "Do Ya Think I'm Disco?," a ditty he'd cowritten to the tune of Rod Stewart's disco hit, "Do Ya Think I'm Sexy?"

Dahl's lyrics:

I wear tight pants, I always stuff a sock in
It always makes the ladies start to talkin'
My shirt is open, I never use the buttons
So I look hip, I work for E.F. Hutton

After that, "all hell broke loose," Morris recalled to the *Times*. "[Fans] charged the field and started tearing up the pitching rubber and the dirt. They took the bases. They started digging out home plate."

Fans destroyed the batting cage and tried to rip home plate out of its mooring. A fire raged in the outfield, as thousands of drunken fans danced—and fought—around it. Owner Bill Veeck took the microphone from Dahl and pleaded for the fans to vacate the field. Instead, they set more fires and kept fighting.

Detroit television station WDIV (Channel 4) broadcast the doubleheader. During the height of the rioting, announcer George Kell said to his broadcast partner Al Kaline, "Al, this is just un-American."

When police in riot gear showed up, the fans ran off the field. Officers made thirty-nine arrests.

The second game was called off when the umpires declared the field was in no shape for a game. The next day, baseball commissioner Bowie Kuhn ruled the game a forfeit to the Tigers, since the White Sox had failed to provide acceptable playing conditions.

"Last night was just a disaster that I didn't investigate carefully enough," Bill Veeck told the Associated Press the day after one of the worst promotional fiascos in baseball history.

THE TIGERS WEREN'T FINISHED dealing with craziness in Chicago. The following season in Comiskey Park, a newly acquired Detroit Tiger got into legal trouble after charging the mound and sparking a massive brawl.

On May 27, 1980, Al Cowens was traded to the Tigers for first baseman Jason Thompson. Like teammates Ron LeFlore and Steve Kemp, Thompson was a solid player who reportedly never meshed with manager Sparky Anderson.

Cowens had been a good ballplayer. In 1977, he finished second to Minnesota Twins second baseman Rod Carew in the American League Most Valuable Player voting. That year, Cowens hit .312 with 23 home runs and 112 RBIs while playing Gold Glove defense.

In 1979, while playing with the Kansas City Royals, Cowens's jaw was broken by a fastball from Texas Rangers relief pitcher Ed Farmer. When Farmer visited him in his hospital room that night, Cowens told him through his wired-shut jaws he thought the pitch had been intentional.

The injury kept Cowens out for three weeks, and when he returned, he wore a protective mask attached to his helmet.

On the night of June 20, 1980, in Comiskey Park, the new Tiger Cowens faced Farmer, who'd been traded to the White Sox. In their first meeting since the beaning, Cowens led off the eleventh inning of a 3–3 tie. Cowens hit a routine ground ball to the shortstop. But instead of running to first base, Cowens charged the mound and tackled Farmer from behind.

"Cowens jumped on him and began punching him in the head," the *Detroit Free Press* reported. "About a half-dozen White Sox immediately piled on Cowens. Then both benches emptied. [Catcher Lance] Parrish was the first Tiger to arrive; [Tiger outfielder Champ] Summers was second, and [Tiger first baseman Richie] Hebner third. Summers got in a good punch at a Chicago coach."

Order was restored, and Cowens was ejected from the game. The fight may have stirred up the Tiger players, who scored two runs in the eleventh inning and held the Sox scoreless in the bottom of the inning to secure the 5–3 win.

As expected, Cowens was suspended for seven games for the incident. What wasn't expected: White Sox owner Bill Veeck called the police and tried to have Cowens arrested for assault and battery.

"Manager Sparky Anderson wouldn't allow police looking for Cowens into the Tiger clubhouse Friday night, and Cowens foiled Veeck's attempts Saturday by taking a morning flight back to Detroit after spending the night in an airport hotel," the *Detroit News* reported.

Neither Veeck nor Farmer was willing to let it go. Farmer told a *Chicago Sun-Times* reporter that he planned to file assault and battery charges against Cowens. Farmer called Cowens's weeklong suspension "a joke," adding, "they probably should have suspended him for the rest of the year."

Veeck agreed. "It was an attack against an unprotected man," he told the *Sun-Times*.

Dave Phillips, the chief of the umpiring crew that was working the Tiger– White Sox series, said he was surprised by Farmer's vow to press charges. "They have these fights all the time," the ump told the *Sun-Times*. "It was totally unwarranted, but it's a joke when they try to arrest a guy."

Veeck promised to have Cowens arrested the next time the Tigers visited Chicago, but that never happened. When the White Sox came to Detroit in September, *News* columnist Joe Falls asked Farmer if he'd bury the hatchet with Cowens if the Tiger outfielder agreed to shake his hand. Cowens agreed, and before the game, the two men met on the field and shook hands.

"It was not easy for Farmer to accept Cowens' handshake, and it was not easy for Cowens to offer it," Falls wrote. "But they showed some great maturity…both men stand very tall today."

ABOUT THE AUTHOR

George Hunter has covered crime for the *Detroit News* for more than twenty years. He's familiar with the subject; he grew up in the Cass Corridor, one of Detroit's most impoverished, crime-ridden neighborhoods, and three of his siblings were Detroit cops. Hunter has appeared in several true-crime documentaries and on news outlets including CNN, Fox News Channel, HLN, the BBC, Japan's Fugi Network and Germany's *Der Spiegel*. Hunter is also a lifelong Detroit Tiger fan, having attended his first game at Tiger Stadium in 1970.